MARZANO RESEARCH DEVELOPMENT TEAM

Director of Publications
Julia A. Simms

Production Editor
Laurel Hecker

Editorial Assistants / Staff Writers
Ming Lee Newcomb

Elizabeth A. Bearden

Marzano Research Associates

Tina H. Boogren

Bev Clemens

Jane Doty Fischer

Jeff Flygare

Tammy Heflebower

Mitzi Hoback

Jan K. Hoegh

Russell Jenson

Jessica Kanold-McIntyre

Sonny Magaña

Margaret McInteer

Diane E. Paynter

Kristin Poage

Salle Quackenboss

Cameron Rains

Tom Roy

Gerry Varty

Phil Warrick

Kenneth C. Williams

ACKNOWLEDGMENTS

I want to thank my former coworkers in Springfield, Ohio, for their guidance during the two years I spent working at a day-treatment center with them. I was fresh out of undergrad and was in charge of managing groups and facilitating lessons on a variety of social-emotional topics. The support of my coworkers helped me realize my interest in classroom climate and behavior management, and I'm happy to share that knowledge in this book.

I also want to thank two of my professors at the University of Oregon, Dr. Kenneth W. Merrell and Dr. Teri Lewis-Palmer. Dr. Merrell's influence and guidance lives with me each day as I pursue my career. Dr. Lewis-Palmer showed me how classroom management can be fun, engaging, and—most importantly—effective.

Finally, I want to thank the publications department at Marzano Research. The feedback I received from Katie Rogers, Julia Simms, and Laurel Hecker helped shape this book into a user-friendly and practical piece.

CONTENTS

Reproducibles are in italics.

CHAPTER 3

ESTABLISHING PROCEDURES AND STRUCTURE 37

CHAPTER 4

REINFORCING EXPECTATIONS 49

ABOUT THE AUTHOR

 Jason E. Harlacher, PhD, is a researcher, consultant, and adjunct professor with over ten years of education experience. He works full time as a senior researcher at Marzano Research in Denver, Colorado, and is coauthor of the Practitioner's Guide to Curriculum-Based Evaluation in Reading. Prior to joining Marzano Research, Dr. Harlacher worked as a school psychologist, a response to intervention (RTI) consultant, and the state director for Positive Behavior Support–Nevada. He presents nationally on schoolwide prevention models and has published articles on RTI, social-emotional learning, and classroom interventions for attention deficit hyperactivity disorder. Dr. Harlacher earned a bachelor's degree in psychology from Ohio University, a master's degree in school psychology from Utah State University, and a doctorate in school psychology from the University of Oregon.

ABOUT MARZANO RESEARCH

Marzano Research is a joint venture between Solution Tree and Dr. Robert J. Marzano. Marzano Research combines Dr. Marzano's forty years of educational research with continuous action research in all major areas of schooling in order to provide effective and accessible instructional strategies, leadership strategies, and classroom assessment strategies that are always at the forefront of best practice. By providing such an all-inclusive research-into-practice resource center, Marzano Research provides teachers and principals with the tools they need to effect profound and immediate improvement in student achievement.

FOREWORD

By Robert J. Marzano

Over the past forty years, I have worked to synthesize educational research and provide practical strategies and techniques that teachers can put to use in their classrooms. This is because I firmly believe that the single most important controllable factor affecting student achievement is the classroom teacher. Effective teaching has a clear and significant impact on student achievement; however, the elements and dynamics involved in effective teaching can be more complex to understand.

I believe that an effective teacher performs three major roles: (1) selecting and employing effective instructional strategies, (2) designing and implementing curriculum that facilitates student learning, and (3) using effective classroom management techniques. While all three roles are critical, the first two are built on a foundation of effective classroom management techniques. Quite simply, effective teaching and learning cannot occur in a poorly managed classroom.

In 2003, I personally investigated the research on classroom management. I found that effective use of classroom management techniques decreased disruptions in classrooms. Furthermore, when teachers employed effective management techniques, student achievement scores increased. These findings raise a very natural question: is it possible to improve one's classroom management techniques? The answer is unequivocally yes. Four decades of educational research provide clear guidance as to the critical elements and aspects of effective classroom management. Teachers who understand specific research-based strategies and techniques and implement them in their classrooms can positively affect student behavior and student achievement.

In the latest book in *The Classroom Strategies Series*, Jason Harlacher provides a clear, convenient guide to strategies that will help teachers create a proactive, positive system of classroom management. Grounded in research and theory, Harlacher's approach walks teachers through the main components of creating a safe, orderly, and well-managed classroom. Additionally, this book provides many practical, ready-to-use resources in the form of reproducible templates that teachers can use to scaffold their implementation of the recommended strategies. Throughout the text, Harlacher also emphasizes the idea of data-driven planning and intervention, giving teachers tools to collect and utilize data to address behavior issues in their classrooms.

Based on my research and the research of others, I truly believe that every teacher can achieve effective classroom management, which, in turn, forms a strong foundation for effective instruction and learning. The key is to know which strategies and techniques are effective and to put those into practice. Here, Harlacher has created a guide to those strategies and techniques that is easily digestible and immediately useful.

INTRODUCTION

Designing Effective Classroom Management is part of a series of books collectively referred to as *The Classroom Strategies Series*. This series aims to provide teachers, as well as building and district administrators, with an in-depth treatment of research-based instructional strategies that can be used in the classroom to enhance student achievement. Many of the strategies addressed in this series have been covered in other works, such as *Classroom Instruction That Works* (Marzano, Pickering, & Pollock, 2001), *Classroom Management That Works* (Marzano, 2003), *The Art and Science of Teaching* (Marzano, 2007), and *Effective Supervision* (Marzano, Frontier, & Livingston, 2011). Although those works devoted a chapter or a part of a chapter to particular strategies, *The Classroom Strategies Series* devotes an entire book to an instructional strategy or set of related strategies.

We begin with a brief but inclusive chapter that reviews the research and theory on effective classroom management. Although you may be eager to move right into those chapters that provide recommendations for practice in schools, we strongly encourage you to examine the research and theory, as it is the foundation for the entire book. Indeed, a basic purpose of *Designing Effective Classroom Management* and others in *The Classroom Strategies Series* is to present the most useful strategies based on the strongest research and theory available.

Because research and theory can provide only a general direction for classroom practice, *Designing Effective Classroom Management* goes one step further to translate that research into applications for classroom management in schools. Specifically, this book outlines a proactive approach to classroom management. In the same way that teachers directly teach academic content, they can also directly teach behavioral expectations. Since students do not all necessarily come to school with the same understanding of appropriate behavior, teachers can prevent inappropriate behavior by actively teaching students what is expected of them. This book presents step-by-step guidelines and specific strategies related to five research-based components of a proactive approach to classroom management.

Following a discussion of the context, research, and theory related to classroom management in chapter 1, chapters 2 through 6 each present a component of effective classroom management:

- Creating and teaching expectations and rules (chapter 2)
- Establishing procedures and structure (chapter 3)
- Reinforcing expectations (chapter 4)

- Actively engaging students (chapter 5)

- Managing misbehavior (chapter 6)

Taken together, these components constitute an approach to classroom management that is designed to help most students behave appropriately in the classroom. However, to address individual students who still struggle to meet expectations, chapter 7 reviews strategies that teachers can use with students who need more individualized attention to be successful in school settings.

How to Use This Book

Educators can use *Designing Effective Classroom Management* as a self-study text that provides an in-depth understanding of effective behavior management in the classroom. Each chapter explains steps and strategies to implement one component of a proactive approach to classroom management. As you progress through the chapters, you will also encounter comprehension questions. It is important to complete these questions and compare your answers with those in the appendix (page 123). Such interaction provides a review of the content and allows a thorough examination of your understanding. Groups or teams of teachers and administrators who wish to examine the topic of classroom management in depth may also use *Designing Effective Classroom Management*. When this is the case, teams should answer the questions independently and then compare their answers in small- or large-group settings.

Chapter 1

RESEARCH AND THEORY

Classroom management is arguably one of the most challenging areas teachers must address. A teacher's level of skill with classroom management is critical to his or her effectiveness in the classroom. This makes intuitive sense—in order for students to learn, the classroom must run smoothly—and research has identified a number of specific benefits associated with effective classroom management. Research has suggested that effective classroom management can help teachers foster a safe and orderly environment in their schools and can reduce rates of misbehavior, bullying, and unsafe behavior (Bradshaw, Koth, Bevans, Ialongo, & Leaf, 2008; Bradshaw, Mitchell, & Leaf, 2010; Horner et al., 2009; Taylor-Greene et al., 1997). These findings are particularly salient given the prevalence of school violence in the United States. In 2011, 12 percent of high school students reported being involved in a physical fight at school (Centers for Disease Control and Prevention [CDC], 2012). On average, bullying involves one-third of students (Otieno & Choongo, 2008), with 10 percent of victims reporting weekly assaults (Nansel et al., 2001). Moreover, school violence is not limited to students: 7 percent of teachers reported being threatened or physically attacked by a student (CDC, 2012), and almost 10 percent of teachers reported acts of student disrespect beyond verbal abuse (Robers, Kemp, Truman, & Snyder, 2013).

Research has also suggested that effective classroom management lays a foundation for students' academic success (Anhalt, McNeil, & Bahl, 1998; Bradshaw et al., 2010; Horner et al., 2009; Musti-Rao & Haydon, 2011). Indeed, one of the strongest rationales for improving one's classroom management ability is that it influences student achievement. Researcher John Hattie (2009) synthesized results from over 800 meta-analyses and identified a number of factors related to classroom management that impact student achievement. Table 1.1 (page 4) displays the factors and their corresponding effect sizes.

As shown in table 1.1, Hattie (2009) calculated effect sizes for several classroom management–related factors. An *effect size* is a statistical measure describing the expected effect of a practice or intervention on students. An effect size of 0.20—considered small (Cohen, 1988)—is equivalent to a percentile gain of eight points. In other words, a student at the 50th percentile who received an intervention with an effect size of 0.20 would be expected to move to the 58th percentile. An effect size of 0.50, considered moderate, is associated with a 19-percentile-point gain, and an effect size of 0.80, considered large, is associated with a percentile-point gain of 29.

Table 1.1: Effect of Selected Classroom Management–Related Factors on Academic Achievement

Classroom Management–Related Factor	Effect Size	Percentile Gain
Tangible recognition	0.82	29
Feedback about appropriateness of behavior	1.00	34
Group contingencies	0.98	34
Rules and procedures	0.76	28
Disciplinary interventions	0.91	32
Direct, concrete consequences	0.57	22

Source: Data from Marzano, 2000, as cited in Hattie, 2009.

In addition to Hattie's findings on student achievement, there is evidence that effective classroom management can improve teachers' work environments. Catherine P. Bradshaw, Christine W. Koth, Katherine B. Bevans, Nicholas Ialongo, and Phillip J. Leaf (2008) reported that Positive Behavioral Interventions and Supports (PBIS)—a schoolwide behavior management and discipline framework that includes teaching and reinforcing behavioral expectations—was associated with better organizational health of a school, as well as with the staff's perceived influence on students' academic scores. The authors hypothesized that the enhanced behavior management led teachers to feel more effective and capable of altering students' scores. Bradshaw and her colleagues (2008, 2010) also noted that the use of PBIS can lead to an environment in which teachers feel more inclined to collaborate.

Finally, teachers without the necessary skills and tools to implement effective classroom management may be less likely to remain in the profession. Richard Ingersoll (2002) estimated that nearly one-third of new teachers quit teaching within their first three years of employment, and almost 40 percent leave the profession within five years. As Lisa Gonzalez, Michelle Stallone Brown, and John R. Slate (2008) pointed out, student behavior is one of the top three reasons that new teachers leave the profession (the other two being administrative issues and salary concerns).

Clearly, effective classroom management skills are pivotal to fostering a safe and orderly school environment, academic success for students, positive working conditions for teachers, and high teacher-retention rates. In attempts to cultivate effective classroom management, teachers, schools, and districts have utilized a number of practices and policies over the years. Here, we review several examples of practices and policies that have been found to be ineffective, such as zero-tolerance policies and the use of suspensions and expulsions, or difficult to implement with fidelity, such as individualized behavior plans. We then present a number of practices and policies that have been found to support effective, proactive classroom management.

Zero-Tolerance Policies

Zero-tolerance policies (ZTPs) mandate that specific consequences—typically suspension or expulsion from school—be consistently used to respond to particular student behaviors. ZTPs were originally intended to address severe and unsafe behaviors such as violence, drugs, and weapons in schools. However, schools' use of ZTPs eventually expanded beyond these behaviors (American Psychological Association

[APA] Zero Tolerance Task Force, 2008). Figure 1.1 presents examples of nonviolent, non-drug-related behaviors that have been addressed using ZTPs. Critics of ZTPs point out that these policies often fail to take into account situational contexts, resulting in a one-size-fits-all approach rather than one that takes school contexts and educator expertise into account (APA Zero Tolerance Task Force, 2008).

The well-intended—yet imperfect—reasoning behind ZTPs is twofold. One assumption is that the use of consequences like suspension and expulsion can deter all students from future acts of violence and misbehavior (APA Zero Tolerance Task Force, 2008). A second assumption is that removing violent or misbehaving students from schools creates a safer and healthier learning environment. Unfortunately, the data on ZTPs do not support these assumptions. For one, school suspension generally predicts future misbehavior and suspension; that is, students who are suspended from school are more likely to be suspended again (Bowditch, 1993; Costenbader & Markson, 1998; Mendez, 2003; Mendez & Knoff, 2003; Tobin, Sugai, & Colvin, 1996). If ZTPs were an effective means of discouraging mis-behavior, there would not be a positive association between a first suspension and future suspensions. Additionally, ZTPs are typically associated with lower school-climate ratings, failure of students to graduate on time, and lower academic achievement in schools (APA Zero Tolerance Task Force, 2008; Civil Rights Project & Advancement Project, 2000). Overall, ZTPs have not been found to be effective behavior management strategies.

- Ten-year-old expelled after turning in a small knife that her mother packed with her lunch to cut an apple (APA Zero Tolerance Task Force, 2008)

- Teenager expelled for talking on a cell phone to his mother who was on deployment in Iraq (APA Zero Tolerance Task Force, 2008)

- Five black male students arrested for felony assault after throwing peanuts on the school bus and accidentally hitting the driver (Civil Rights Project & Advancement Project, 2000)

- Six-year-old student suspended for bringing a toenail clipper to school (Civil Rights Project & Advancement Project, 2000)

- Kindergartener suspended for wearing a Halloween costume that included a toy ax (Civil Rights Project & Advancement Project, 2000)

- Teenager expelled after it was discovered that he had left a pocketknife in his backpack after a Boy Scouts camping trip (Civil Rights Project & Advancement Project, 2000)

- Ten-year-old student given numerous multi-day suspensions for violations such as failing to do an assignment, humming while tapping on her desk, and talking back to her teacher (Civil Rights Project & Advancement Project, 2000)

- Seventh-grade student served a nine-day suspension for drug use after sniffing white-out (Civil Rights Project & Advancement Project, 2000)

- Fifth-grade student suspended for one year for possession of a weapon when it was discovered that he had taken razor blades away from a classmate who intended to hurt other students (Civil Rights Project & Advancement Project, 2000)

Figure 1.1: Examples of zero-tolerance policy punishments.

Suspensions and Expulsions

Although suspension and expulsion are related to ZTPs, many schools without ZTPs still rely on sus-pensions and expulsions as primary forms of behavior management. The U.S. Department of Education Office for Civil Rights (OCR; 2014) reported that during the 2011–12 school year, almost two million students were suspended and over one hundred thousand were expelled. Research has shown that such an approach can be problematic. John M. Wallace, Sara Goodkind, Cynthia M. Wallace, and Jerald

G. Bachman (2008) found that suspensions and expulsions increase the amount of time students are left unsupervised because they are often at home while parents or guardians are at work. Additionally, neither suspensions nor expulsions typically provide any instructional component to help students learn new behaviors (Mendez, 2003; Mendez & Knoff, 2003). Finally, the effects of suspension and expulsion frequently extend beyond students' years in school. Students who are suspended are three times more likely to drop out of school, and students who drop out are three times more likely to be incarcerated later in life (Coalition for Juvenile Justice, 2001; Ekstrom, Goertz, Pollack, & Rock, 1986).

The correlation between being suspended or expelled and eventually entering the prison system—sometimes referred to as the "the school-to-prison pipeline" (American Civil Liberties Union, n.d.; Civil Rights Project & Advancement Project, 2000; Lieberman, n.d.)—is especially troubling in light of race, gender, and ability disparities in suspension and expulsion rates. In 2006, Native American, Hispanic, and African American students were respectively 1.52, 1.23, and 2.84 times more likely to be suspended than Caucasian students (APA Zero Tolerance Task Force, 2008). More recent data indicate this trend has not changed, as African American students are still three times more likely to be suspended or expelled than Caucasian students (OCR, 2014), despite there being no difference in actual rates of problem behavior (Skiba, Michael, Nardo, & Peterson, 2002). Suspension and expulsion disparities also extend to students with disabilities (who are more than twice as likely to be suspended as students without disabilities) and to boys (who are roughly twice as likely to be suspended as girls; OCR, 2014).

A number of researchers have found that disparate rates of suspension and expulsion are related to facets of classroom management, including the nature of teacher-student interactions, differences in language and culture, and biases toward certain races and ethnic groups (APA Zero Tolerance Task Force, 2008; Skiba et al., 2002; Vavrus & Cole, 2002; Wallace et al., 2008). Frances Vavrus and KimMarie Cole (2002) examined interactions between students and teachers in a middle school. They found that suspensions were not always preceded by violent acts or other flagrant violations of school policy. Instead, suspensions sometimes resulted from a series of minor offenses—typically the vaguely defined "disruption"—often by multiple students, in which one student was eventually singled out. That is, researchers observed a number of cases in which, despite "the absence of an obvious breach of disciplinary policy" (Vavrus & Cole, 2002, p. 88), teachers resorted to suspending one student out of a group of generally disruptive students without first attempting to control the situation using less aversive (that is, less severe) strategies. In light of these findings and others, it appears that suspension and expulsion are not optimal approaches to promoting effective classroom management.

Individualized Behavior Plans

Individualized behavior plans are interventions designed to manage the behavior of a specific student. Teachers who are struggling with a particular student often request support from experts in the school, such as a psychologist or counselor, or from the student's parents. Sometimes the teacher attends a problem-solving conference or a referral meeting, or a support staff member (for example, a counselor or psychologist) enters the classroom, observes the student, and suggests an individualized solution.

Individualized behavior plans can be powerful, but they can also be cumbersome to implement with fidelity. That is, the amount of time and number of components required often make it difficult for teachers to implement an individualized plan as originally designed or intended (Wolery, 2011). Indeed, Frank M. Gresham (2009) and George H. Noell, Gary J. Duhon, Susan L. Gatti, and James E. Connell (2002) found that behavior plans tend to be implemented with low fidelity, which results in low effectiveness. Additionally, if more than one student in a class needs individualized support, it can be difficult for a single teacher to implement several behavior plans at once. The process of designing and implementing new plans for each behavior issue can create a fragmented, piecemeal approach to behavior management (Kratochwill, Elliott, & Callan-Stoiber, 2002; Kratochwill & Shernoff, 2004). Overall, many teachers find that juggling several plans at a time with the expectation of doing something slightly different for each student is frustrating, demanding, and fairly ineffective (Dunson, Hughes, & Jackson, 1994; Kratochwill et al., 2002; Slonski-Fowler & Truscott, 2004).

In summary, the three practices reviewed here (zero-tolerance policies, suspensions and expulsions, and individualized behavior plans) have one important feature in common: they are reactive. That is, they are typically used in response to behavior issues that have already arisen. As shown in this section, these reactive practices are not often effective. Consequently, many educators and researchers have called for a more proactive approach to classroom management, one that allows for more flexible use of consequences (such as suspension and expulsion), as well as a range of alternative consequences to logically suit different behaviors (APA Zero Tolerance Task Force, 2008; Evans & Lester, 2012; Horner, Sugai, Todd, & Lewis-Palmer, 2005; Skiba, 2010). As Russell Skiba and Reece Peterson (2000) said, "Educators and policy makers must begin to look beyond stiffer consequences to long-term planning designed to foster nonviolent school communities" (p. 341). In other words, instead of using reactive consequences to address misbehavior, educators can plan ahead to prevent problems by using a proactive approach to classroom management.

A Proactive Approach to Classroom Management

Effective classroom management does not consist of simply punishing students for misbehavior. Instead, we recommend a proactive approach that draws from three theoretical principles: (1) behaviorism and applied behavior analysis, (2) direct instruction of desired behaviors, and (3) predictability and structure. Here, we briefly describe each of these underlying principles.

Behaviorism and Applied Behavior Analysis

A key aspect of the psychological theory of *behaviorism* (Skinner, 1953, 1976) is that all behaviors have a functional purpose, serving either to gain something (such as a reward) or to avoid something (such as an adverse situation or penalty). A *behavior* is any observable and measurable act. Since its conception, behaviorism and its principles have been used in various settings through *applied behavior analysis* (ABA; the methodical use of interventions to improve behavior) in order to promote desired behaviors and discourage undesired ones. This approach has been applied in the classroom and can be extremely effective (for example, see Alberto & Troutman, 2013; Baer, Wolf, & Risley, 1968; Wolery, Bailey, & Sugai, 1988). One tenet of ABA is that behavior does not occur in a vacuum (Dunlap, Harrower, & Fox, 2005). Instead, it occurs within a chain of events: behaviors are triggered and then maintained by certain stimuli in the environment (Dunlap et al., 2005; Wolery et al., 1988), as shown in figure 1.2. Understanding the context of a certain behavior allows teachers to intervene to increase desired behaviors and decrease others (Carr et al., 2002; Crone & Horner, 2003; Dunlap et al., 2005). This chain of events is referred to as a *behavior sequence* (Wolery et al., 1988).

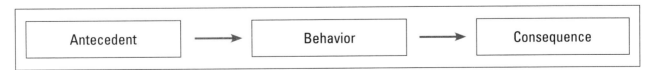

Figure 1.2: Three components of the behavior sequence.

Source: Adapted from Dunlap et al., 2005.

Every behavior is preceded by an *antecedent*, which is the act or incident that triggers the behavior, and is followed by a *consequence*, which influences the likelihood of the behavior happening again. There are two types of consequences: (1) *reinforcement* (events, stimuli, or outcomes that increase rates of behavior), and (2) *punishment* (events, stimuli, or outcomes that decrease rates of behavior; Skinner, 1953, 1976; Watson, 1913; see also Alberto & Troutman, 2013; Baer et al., 1968; Wolery et al., 1988). According to behaviorism, a person learns to use behaviors that lead to reinforcement and avoid the use of behaviors that lead to punishment (Skinner, 1953). Behaviorism also includes the *setting event*, which refers to circumstances and prior events that affect the likelihood that an antecedent will trigger a behavior, as well as the value of a consequence. This book, however, focuses on antecedents, behaviors, and consequences as the simplest and most effective ways to manage behavior in the classroom.

As an example of how the behavior sequence works, imagine a social studies class. The teacher develops a routine with the class in which the signal of the bell to start class prompts students to complete a warm-up activity listed on the whiteboard. The bell acts as an antecedent for the behavior of completing the warm-up activity, and those students who complete the work earn a few minutes of free time at the end of class. In response to the bell (antecedent), student A completes the warm-up activity (desired behavior) and earns free time (reinforcement consequence). However, student B does not complete the warm-up activity (undesired behavior) and has to complete the activity at the end of class instead of having free time (punishment consequence).

Using ABA, teachers can manipulate aspects of the behavior sequence to prevent or alter problem behaviors. Figure 1.3 depicts different types of manipulations that can be used on the antecedent, behavior, or consequence.

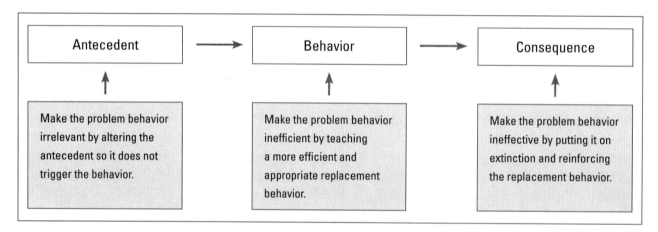

Figure 1.3: The behavior sequence and possible manipulations.

Source: Adapted from Crone & Horner, 2003.

As shown in figure 1.3, the outcome of a manipulation depends on where in the sequence the teacher introduces it (Bambara & Kern, 2005; Crone & Horner, 2003; O'Neil et al., 1997). Manipulation of the antecedent aims to make a behavior *irrelevant*—that is, to lessen the likelihood that the behavior happens in the first place—by removing any event that may trigger it. For instance, if the problem behavior of talking to a peer is triggered by sitting next to a friend, a teacher can move a student's seat. Manipulation of the behavior focuses on teaching a *replacement behavior*, thus rendering the old behavior inefficient and, in turn, less appealing. For example, a teacher might ask a student to write down things she wants to say to friends during class so she can tell them those things later, perhaps during recess or a passing period.

Manipulation of consequences entails two components. The first component involves discouraging an unwanted behavior by withholding reinforcement, thus making it ineffective. Withholding reinforcement for an unwanted behavior until that behavior ceases is called *extinction* (Skinner, 1953; Wolery et al., 1988). The second component involves providing reinforcement for a more desirable replacement behavior. For the manipulation of consequences to be maximally effective, both components should be used together. For example, a teacher can use extinction by ignoring a student who talks out of turn. In this example, the student uses the problem behavior (talking out of turn) to gain reinforcement (the teacher's attention), so the teacher can put it on extinction by removing that reinforcement (ignoring the student when she talks out of turn). Simultaneously, the teacher would provide the student with reinforcement for the replacement behavior of raising her hand, perhaps through verbal praise.

Teaching and reinforcing a replacement behavior can be a fairly complex process. The student's problem behavior is denied reinforcement while, at the same time, planned and natural reinforcements are used to teach and reinforce a replacement behavior. Additionally, a student may be given a temporary behavior that serves the same function as the problem behavior while the student learns the replacement behavior. A temporary behavior is often used when the problem behavior is highly disruptive or dangerous. For example, imagine a student who acts out and destroys property in class when given a difficult assignment. The student tears up the work, yells, and even turns over chairs in order to avoid completing the work. Here, the antecedent of difficult work triggers the problem behavior of acting out in order to escape difficult work. For this situation, the student is avoiding work because he lacks the academic skills needed to complete the work. The desired replacement behavior is for the student to complete work quietly, but the student must be taught missing academic skills in order to use the new behavior. Teaching academic skills can take some time, so a temporary behavior is used in the meantime to prevent the student from being disruptive. In this case, the student might be given a break pass that serves the same function as the problem behavior. Instead of becoming frustrated and starting to yell, tear up work, and cause a disruption, the student can instead hold up a card and earn a ten-minute break. The student's use of the card serves the same function as the problem behavior: the student is able to escape the work. Here, the escape is short; after ten minutes, the student has a conference with the teacher before attempting the work again. The teacher manipulates the consequences in this example by *not* removing the work when the student engages in the problem behavior (that is, the problem behavior is put on extinction), but the student is able to temporarily escape the work by using the break pass (that is, reinforcement for temporary behavior). Finally, the student is praised and rewarded with previously agreed-upon items (for example, extra recess, time to listen to music, and so on) if the student completes a certain amount of work (that is, reinforcement for replacement behavior). Over time, the tangible rewards are phased out and the replacement behavior is maintained by natural reinforcement, such as praise or feeling successful in class. Figure 1.4 (page 10) illustrates how a temporary behavior might be incorporated into the behavior sequence.

The use of ABA has been shown to facilitate the acquisition of new academic behaviors (Daly, Lentz, & Boyer, 1996; Daly & Martens, 1994) as well as social-emotional behaviors (Anhalt et al., 1998; Lewis, Hudson, Richter, & Johnson, 2004; Stormont, Smith, & Lewis, 2007). Understanding the theory of behaviorism and ABA lays the foundation for the next theoretical principle of a proactive approach to classroom management: direct instruction of desired behaviors.

Direct Instruction of Desired Behaviors

Craig Darch and his colleagues (Darch & Kame'enui, 2003; Darch, Miller, & Shippen, 1998) championed the idea that desired behaviors should be taught in the same manner as academics. That is, teachers should adopt an instructional approach to behavior similar to the instructional approach used to teach academic content. In such an approach, knowledge or skills are identified and teachers provide instruction and guidance to help students learn the knowledge or skills. Craig Darch and Ed Kame'enui (2003) contended that teaching behavioral expectations should use a similar process: "The teacher teaches carefully and strategically all that is required so that students have the information necessary to perform or behave appropriately" (p. 3).

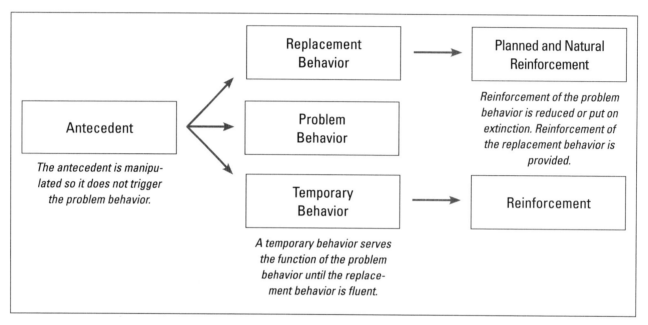

Figure 1.4: Illustration of reducing problem behavior and increasing appropriate replacement behavior.

Source: Adapted from Crone & Horner, 2003.

To illustrate, consider a student who is struggling to understand the meaning of a word. A teacher's immediate reaction would likely be to reteach the word to the student. After all, if the student is struggling to understand a word, it means that knowledge or skills are missing. The role of the teacher is to teach the missing knowledge or skills. Now consider a student who does not meet behavioral expectations; for example, he or she blurts out an answer or is rude to another student. Rather than reteach the appropriate behavior, a teacher might instead punish the student, assuming that the student knows the correct way to act but is choosing to misbehave. Consider the following quote from John Herner (1998), former president of the National Association of State Directors of Special Education:

> If a child doesn't know how to read, we teach.
> If a child doesn't know how to swim, we teach.
> If a child doesn't know how to multiply, we teach.
> If a child doesn't know how to drive, we teach.
> If a child doesn't know how to behave, we . . . punish? (p. 2)

We agree with Darch and colleagues' (1998) assertion that behavior ought to be directly taught to students in the same manner as academics. In short, misbehavior is an opportunity to teach, not to punish.

When a teacher identifies a target behavior, he or she models it for students, provides opportunities to practice it, and then gives positive reinforcement to students who use the behavior. The practice of teaching and reinforcing behaviors to students has been effective at the classroom level (Anhalt et al., 1998; DePry & Sugai, 2002; Filcheck, McNeil, Greco, & Bernard, 2004) and at the schoolwide level in both elementary (Bradshaw et al., 2010; Taylor-Greene et al., 1997) and secondary schools (Bohanon et al., 2006; Bradshaw et al., 2010).

Predictability and Structure

The final foundational principle for effective classroom management is a predictable and clear structure within the classroom. As Harry Wong and Rosemary Wong pointed out in their 2009 book *The First Days of School*, consistency is an essential ingredient for classroom management. Classrooms with clear structure and procedures are ones in which academic learning time is maximized, downtime is minimal, and students know exactly what to do and when to do it. In fact, James Stronge, Thomas Ward, and Leslie Grant (2011) examined the differences between classrooms with low-achieving students and those with high-achieving students. They found that in classrooms with higher achievement, teachers had better classroom management than those in classrooms with lower achieving students. Specifically, teachers in high-achieving classrooms established routines for their students, monitored student behavior, and used time efficiently (see also Stronge, Ward, Tucker, & Hindman, 2008).

If teachers do not provide expectations, structure, and routine, students are forced to guess what to do, and they may not make decisions conducive to a safe and orderly environment. Stephanie Campbell and Christopher Skinner (2004) illustrated this point with a study that taught students to transition more quickly after lunch. Originally, the teacher did not have a clear routine for when students returned to the classroom following lunch. As they milled about in the classroom waiting for the next activity to begin, the students would become disruptive and engage in problem behavior. After the students learned a clear transition routine and received reinforcement for adhering to it, the transition time and amount of problem behavior decreased substantially. No longer left alone to figure out what to do or to entertain themselves, the students in the study were less likely to become disruptive. When students are given clear routines and guidelines, they are more likely to display appropriate behavior (Horner et al., 2005). Therefore, classrooms should be built on ensuring predictability and structure.

Five Practical Components of Effective Classroom Management

Drawing on the theoretical base provided by behavioral theory, direct instruction, and predictability and structure, the remainder of this chapter presents research on particular elements of a well-managed classroom. Specifically, we take a closer look at three comprehensive literature reviews on the subject, the results of which were summarized by Julie Greenberg, Hannah Putman, and Kate Walsh (2014) in a report from the National Council on Teacher Quality (NCTQ).

The first literature review—conducted by Brandi Simonsen, Sarah Fairbanks, Amy Briesch, Diane Myers, and George Sugai (2008)—examined experimental studies that demonstrated effective classroom practices. In this review, the authors focused on classroom management practices that had at least three empirical studies to support their use. Altogether, they identified twenty general classroom management practices, which they organized into five categories.

1. Maximize structure and predictability

2. Post, teach, review, monitor, and reinforce expectations

3. Actively engage students in observable ways

4. Use a continuum of strategies to acknowledge appropriate behavior

5. Use a continuum of strategies to respond to inappropriate behavior

The second review of classroom management practices, which identified effective strategies similar to those described by Simonsen and her colleagues (2008), was a practice guide published by the Institute of Education Sciences (IES). In the IES guide, Michael Epstein, Marc Atkins, Douglas Cullinan, Krista Kutash, and Robin Weaver (2008) examined the literature on classroom management and evaluated the strength of evidence for certain practices. They rated the evidence supporting each practice as low, moderate, or strong, describing strong evidence as "consistent and generalizable evidence that an intervention strategy or program causes an improvement in behavioral outcomes" (p. 2). They identified the following practices as those supported by strong evidence: (1) teaching expectations and skills to students, (2) reinforcing those expectations and skills, and (3) increasing student engagement by ensuring students are academically successful with the material and have multiple opportunities to respond.

The third study was an updated review of classroom practices conducted by Regina Oliver, Joseph Wehby, and Daniel Reschly (2011), which included effect sizes for specific classroom management practices. In the review, the authors examined *universal classroom management*, which they defined as "a collection of non-instructional classroom procedures implemented by teachers in classroom settings with all students for the purposes of teaching prosocial behavior as well as preventing and reducing inappropriate behavior" (pp. 7–8). They wanted to find out the extent to which universal classroom management could reduce disruptive behavior. They calculated an effect size of .80, which (as mentioned previously) is considered a large effect and equivalent to a 29-percentile-point gain. They concluded that teachers who use universal classroom management practices can expect a significant reduction of disruptive, inappropriate, or aggressive behavior from students.

Based on these reviews, Greenberg and her colleagues (2014) synthesized the most important elements of an effective classroom management program. They asserted that a classroom management plan could greatly reduce student behavior issues if it incorporated the components they identified in these three literature reviews. They presented the following five steps.

1. Teach expectations directly.

2. Establish procedures and structure.

3. Reinforce the previously taught expectations.

4. Actively engage students.

5. Manage misbehavior.

Table 1.2 briefly describes and exemplifies each of these five components and indicates which of the three reviews supports its use. The order in which these five components are listed signifies hierarchical importance. The first strategy—teaching expectations—can be considered foundational to the other components in table 1.2, which all build upon teaching expectations. This is meant to discourage teachers from trying to manage misbehavior without first establishing the other four components (teaching expectations, establishing procedures and structure, reinforcing previously taught expectations, and actively engaging students).

These five components of effective classroom management are further supported by the work of a number of education researchers and theorists, many of whom have championed similar management strategies in the past. Indeed, many researchers and theorists have called for direct instruction in classroom expectations (Canter, 2010; Fay & Funk, 1995; Horner et al., 2005, 2009; Marzano, 2003; Taylor-Greene et al., 1997; Wong & Wong, 2009), establishing clear routines and procedures (Hattie, 2009; Marzano, 2003; Stronge et al., 2011; Wong & Wong, 2009), reinforcing classroom expectations

(Alberto & Troutman, 2013; Deitz & Repp, 1973, 1983; Feldman, 2003; Flora, 2000; Horner et al., 2005, 2009; Taylor-Greene et al., 1997; Wolery et al., 1988), actively engaging students (Brophy & Good, 1986; Carnine, 1976; Haydon et al., 2010; Haydon, Mancil, & Van Loan, 2009; Heward, 1994, 1997; Sutherland & Wehby, 2001), and using a variety of methods to manage misbehavior (Alberto & Troutman, 2013; DePry & Sugai, 2002; Foxx & Bechtel, 1982; Hattie, 2009; Wolery et al., 1988).

Table 1.2: Five Classroom Management Components Identified in Three Literature Reviews

Classroom Management Component	Description	Example	Supporting Reviews
Teach expectations directly.	Teachers provide explicit, direct instruction about their expectations for students.	The teacher leads whole-class lessons on what responsibility looks like in different school settings (for example, small-group, independent work time, hallway, and so on).	Epstein et al., 2008 Oliver et al., 2011 Simonsen et al., 2008
Establish procedures and structure.	Students are explicitly taught the procedures for certain activities. The physical layout of the classroom also contributes to effective structure.	A teacher establishes procedures for handing in homework that ensure an orderly and structured environment.	Oliver et al., 2011 Simonsen et al., 2008
Reinforce the previously taught expectations.	Students' behavior is rewarded when they meet classroom expectations.	Students receive verbal praise and small tickets. These tickets are then used to purchase items from a classroom store.	Epstein et al., 2008 Oliver et al., 2011
Actively engage students.	Teachers ensure that students are engaged in tasks and academically successful.	The teacher uses four to six choral responses per minute during whole-class instruction.	Epstein et al., 2008 Oliver et al., 2011 Simonsen et al., 2008
Manage misbehavior.	Teachers use a variety of nonaversive strategies to decrease rates of problematic behavior.	A teacher uses overcorrection for lining up after the class has difficulty lining up appropriately.	Oliver et al., 2011 Simonsen et al., 2008

Source: Adapted from Greenberg et al., 2014.

Despite the importance of implementing these five components of classroom management, many teacher training programs do not prioritize them. New teachers typically graduate with some knowledge of classroom management; however, most are not fully equipped with current, relevant, and research-based instruction on the subject. In their NCTQ report, Greenberg and her colleagues (2014) examined the level of training that preservice teachers received in these five components of effective classroom management. While most teacher training programs (97 percent) offered some amount of instruction on classroom management, an average program only covered half of these five areas. Only 21 percent of the programs covered all five. Furthermore, a mere 15 percent of the programs provided a full course on classroom management, complete with assigned readings and a class period dedicated to the subject. This inconsistent level of preparation in classroom management means that many teachers leave their training programs without a clear understanding of effective management practices.

Summary

To create a safe, orderly, and productive classroom environment, teachers can adopt a proactive approach grounded in foundational theoretical principles and supported by empirical research (see table 1.2, page 13). Teachers who use this approach can create and teach expectations and rules, establish procedures and structure, reinforce expectations, actively engage students, manage misbehavior, and address the unique needs of individual students who struggle to meet expectations. The subsequent chapters elaborate on these six areas and offer practical steps for the implementation and use of each in the classroom.

Chapter 2

CREATING AND TEACHING EXPECTATIONS AND RULES

Broadly defined, *expectations* are general guidelines for behavior that apply to all students and all routines within the classroom. General expectations create a foundation of values and social skills that teachers can draw upon when developing specific rules for various events within the classroom. This idea of broad expectations is a common concept among researchers and educators (for example, Anhalt et al., 1998; Darch & Kame'enui, 2003; Horner et al., 2005; Sailor, Dunlap, Sugai, & Horner, 2009; Taylor-Greene et al., 1997; Wong & Wong, 2009). For example, the Positive Behavioral Interventions and Supports (PBIS) model was developed on the foundation of teaching broad expectations to all students as an alternative to the historical use of punitive and aversive measures for behavior management (Carr et al., 2002; Sailor et al., 2009). Additionally, Jim Fay and David Funk (authors of 1995's *Teaching With Love and Logic*) encouraged teachers to develop broad expectations for behavior and help students understand their associated rationale, logic, and consequences:

> Perhaps it would be better to have the class governed by a set of values that can apply in numerous situations, principles that consider personalities and experiences, and "rules" that leave adults with more opportunity to develop strategies that work with individual students. (p. 107)

To illustrate the application of expectations in a classroom, consider an expectation such as "Be responsible." This expectation can apply to many different activities, locations, and routines. Students are expected to be responsible during group work (for example, "Contribute to the group discussion"), in the lunchroom (for example, "Throw away your trash"), and during a lining-up routine (for example, "Push in your chair after standing up"). *Rules*, on the other hand, are more specific; they apply to particular activities or routines. While the rule "Focus on your own work" does pertain to being responsible, it only applies in the context of certain routines and activities—it is a useful rule in the context of classroom work but is not, for instance, a relevant rule during lunchtime. Teachers develop expectations and corresponding rules for given settings in order to teach students the behavior expected of them.

When creating a set of school or classroom expectations, teachers can utilize the following three-step process:

1. Identify and clearly express general expectations.

2. Create rules for specific events using an events-expectations matrix.

3. Actively teach the expectations and rules.

The next sections describe each step in this process.

Identify and Clearly Express General Expectations

The first step in teaching expectations to students is to identify the expectations themselves. As previously explained, expectations apply to all events within the classroom and specify general criteria for success in those events.

Teachers can identify expectations in a number of different ways. For one, teachers might create a set of classroom expectations before the school year begins. One way to do this involves examining the school's mission statement and identifying expectations that align with it. Consider the following mission statement:

> Student success at Wrigley Middle School means high expectations for all; differentiated, rigorous instruction; and a safe environment created by students who always demonstrate personal responsibility and respect for others.

A brief analysis of this statement reveals that Wrigley Middle School values qualities such as safety, responsibility, respect, integrity, and equality. Using these values, a teacher can create expectations that align with the school's mission statement. Alternatively, teachers can simply consider the kinds of traits that a student needs to be successful in the classroom or school environment and base classroom expectations on those characteristics. First, create a list of the behaviors and attitudes of successful students (such as attentiveness, autonomy, organization, and so on), eliminate duplicates, and sort them into categories (Florida's Positive Behavior Support Project, n.d.). Then, use the categories to form expectations.

A second option involves gathering input from students about expectations. Research has shown that students are more likely to follow and respect a teacher's expectations if they have had some level of participation in creating them (Gable, Hester, Rock, & Hughes, 2009; Marzano, 2003). This approach is particularly effective for secondary students (Buluc, 2006). To involve students, a teacher might lead a class discussion about behavior. Begin by asking students how people should generally behave in school in order for everyone to learn and feel safe. Next, have students break into small groups and list specific behaviors. Prompt students to eliminate or combine redundant behaviors and then list the top three behaviors from each group on the board. Discuss each behavior as a class, combining redundant behaviors and eliminating irrelevant ones in order to reduce the number of individual items on the list. Finally, identify the most important behaviors from the list and use them to form expectations. It is important to note that while this approach may encourage more student buy-in, it also delays the active teaching of expectations until after students generate them.

The final way to identify expectations involves analyzing classroom behavior data, identifying the most prevalent problem behaviors, and constructing a customized list of expectations to address those behaviors. To use this method, teachers can either refer to pre-existing data (such as office discipline referrals) or gather new data through direct classroom observations. If data is not yet available for the current school year (perhaps because it is the beginning of the year), a teacher could analyze data from the previous year. Although those students are no longer in the classroom, it may be a good place to start for identifying expectations. Pre-existing data can include office discipline referrals, phone calls home for behavior, or any other form of data that summarizes the nature and frequency of a problem behavior. When analyzing pre-existing data, the goal is to search for patterns. Consider figure 2.1, which charts all of the discipline referrals for a classroom during the first several months of school.

As shown in figure 2.1, the behaviors that received the most referrals include disruption, disrespect, plagiarism, and verbal aggression. Consequently, a teacher may decide to focus on creating expectations around respect (for disrespectful behavior and verbal aggression), responsibility (for disruption), and honesty (for plagiarism) in order to specifically target these problem behaviors. Although typical expectations (for example, be safe, be respectful, be responsible) will encompass many problem behaviors, using data can help identify hidden problems or expectations that need extra emphasis.

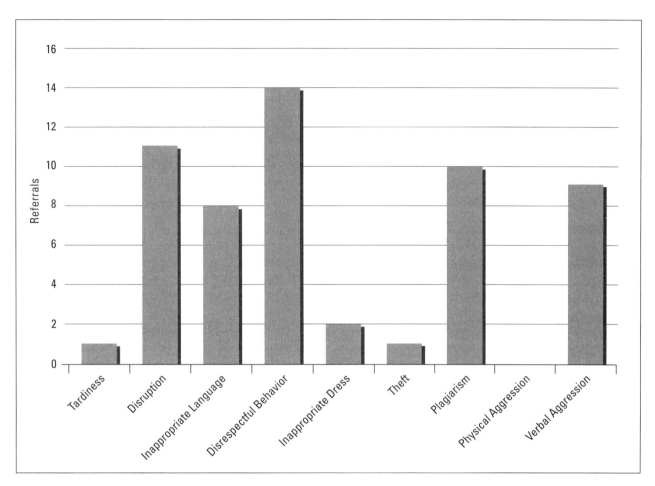

Figure 2.1: Office discipline referrals for various behaviors in a middle school classroom.

If pre-existing data will not suffice, a teacher may wish to observe his or her own classroom and collect current data. Because observing and documenting problem behavior while actively teaching can be cumbersome, ask one or more colleagues to conduct brief observations of the classroom to identify behavioral issues. Collecting observational data is most applicable after the school year has started or when the teacher has noticed an increase in problematic behavior. Ideally, teachers create classroom management plans and expectations at the beginning of the school year, teach expectations to students starting on the first day of school, and then use observations to adjust expectations if student behavior becomes problematic later on.

To conduct observations of behavior, first determine which behaviors to observe and operationally define each one. In other words, create definitions that clearly and unambiguously describe the exact actions of each behavior. This ensures accuracy of the data and avoids confusion as to the exact nature of the behavior. For instance, telling a parent or administrator that a student can't sit still provides almost no information on the frequency, intensity, or severity of the behavior. However, if a teacher operationally defines "can't sit still" as "The student stays completely in his seat, with all four chair legs and his two feet on the floor, for only three minutes at a time during a fifty-minute class period," then he or she provides a much better description of the behavior.

Operational definitions also ensure accuracy of behavior data. When observing behavior, each student action should be recorded in only one category of behavior. If the categories of behavior are not well defined, it may be difficult to decide where a student's specific action should be recorded. For example, if a student calls a peer a name, that action could be considered "Disrespectful to peer" or "Inappropriate language." The more specifically each category is defined, the more easily and accurately the observer will be able to record behavioral data. Teachers should strive to define behaviors with enough detail to make them as mutually exclusive as possible. Note, however, that some judgment calls by the teacher or observer will still be necessary. Table 2.1 lists operationalized definitions for some typical problem behaviors; teachers should feel free to define, observe, and record additional types of behaviors.

Table 2.1: Operational Definitions and Examples for Problem Behaviors

Behavior	Operational Definition	Example
Defiance	The student willfully does not follow or respond to adult requests within five seconds of receiving them.	The teacher asks the student to take his seat and the student continues to walk around the room.
Disrespect to Teacher	The student is rude to a teacher or speaks in a condescending or contentious manner.	The student mutters a negative statement under her breath and rolls her eyes.
Disrespect to Peer	The student is rude or makes derogatory comments to a classmate.	The student says, "Duh!" after a classmate answers a question incorrectly.
Disruption	The student engages in behavior that interrupts a lesson or activity, such as untimely noisemaking, roughhousing, or sustained out-of-seat behavior.	The student loudly and repeatedly taps a pencil on her desk during a silent reading activity.
Physical Contact	The student makes bodily contact with another student in an inappropriate way.	The student invades another student's space by bumping into the student while lining up.
Physical Aggression	The student pushes, shoves, hits, kicks, or is in some way violent toward a classmate.	The student says, "Watch it!" and shoves a classmate out of his way while lining up.
Inappropriate Language	The student communicates using vulgar or derogatory speech, gestures, or writing.	The student uses profanity when talking to a classmate.
Property Misuse	The student intentionally uses property or materials in a destructive or improper manner.	The student forces pens into the pencil sharpener.
Tardiness	The student arrives late to class or is not seated when the bell rings.	Two students are standing in the hallway talking when the bell rings.
Technology Violation	The student uses a cell phone, computer, camera, or other form of technology inappropriately.	A student is watching sports highlight videos in the computer lab during class instead of completing work.

Source: Adapted from Todd, Horner, & Tobin, 2006.

If a teacher asks a colleague to observe, that person might conduct several five- to ten-minute observations of the class over a period of one to two weeks. Observations need not be formal; observers can stop in and leave at their convenience. During an observation, the colleague can use "Conducting Observations to Identify Expectations" (page 32) to record a tally at each instance of problem behavior, indicating which type of behavior has occurred and how often. Next, compare the occurrences of each problem behavior to determine which ones occur most frequently. To make the patterns easier to interpret, teachers can organize the information in a bar chart such as the one in figure 2.1 (page 17). Finally, examine the behaviors that occur most frequently and create expectations to respond to them.

Teachers can use a few guidelines when writing expectations for students. First, limit the number of expectations to between three and five. Fewer than three general expectations won't cover the breadth of behavior within a classroom, and more than five can create redundancies and be difficult for students to remember (Gable et al., 2009; Horner et al., 2005; McGinnis, Frederick, & Edwards, 1995; Taylor-Greene et al., 1997).

Second, state expectations in positive terms: tell students what *to do*, rather than what *not to do* (Gable et al., 2009; Horner et al., 2005; McGinnis et al., 1995). For example, the expectation "Be considerate" is preferable to a statement such as "Don't be rude." A helpful hint to remember when writing positively phrased expectations is that if a sleeping person could comply with the statement, the expectation is probably not very useful.

Third, state the expectations in simple language (Gable et al., 2009). That is, use short phrases and describe broad yet actionable ideas. For example, use "Be ready" instead of "Be sure you have all materials for your work," or say "Welcome others" rather than "Say hello and wave to classroom visitors." Using simple language will also make it easier for students to remember the expectations (Gable et al., 2009; Taylor-Geene et al., 1997). Finally, use action-oriented words that can easily translate into specific behaviors (Canter, 2010; Darch & Kame'enui, 2003; Wong & Wong, 2009). This guideline is very important because the expectations will be translated into specific rules for different events in the classroom (which is discussed later in this chapter). For example, the expectation "Be safe" can encompass more concrete rules such as "Keep your hands to yourself" and "Use playground equipment appropriately." If the expectation is too specific, such as "Sit in your seat," it cannot be translated into more specific rules and it may not be applicable in all settings (for example, "Sit in your seat" does not apply to waiting at the bus stop). At the same time, an expectation such as "diversity" is not actionable; it does not lend itself to specific rules (that is, students cannot demonstrate it by performing specific actions during various activities). Table 2.2 (page 20) lists guidelines and compares examples and non-examples of effective expectations.

Additionally, some teachers choose to create expectations based on an acronym or the school's mascot. For example, a teacher might use the mnemonic *high five* and have five expectations: (1) safe, (2) responsible, (3) respectful, (4) ready, and (5) productive. This teacher can remind students of the expectations by raising his or her hand and saying, "Give me five!" Other teachers might use their school's mascot—for example, the Hawks—and create expectations for each letter: **H**ave respect, **A**ct responsibly, **W**ork honestly, **K**eep trying, **S**upport others (see Taylor-Greene et al., 1997). Still others might use a term related to their school or mascot. For example, a school whose mascot is a bear might use PAWS: be **P**rompt, **A**ccept responsibility, **W**ork hard, **S**how respect.

Table 2.2: Guidelines, Examples, and Nonexamples for Expectations

Guidelines	Examples	Nonexamples
Limit a list of expectations to between three and five.	Be prepared. Demonstrate integrity. Show empathy.	Have fun. Be safe. Make friends. Take care of things. Mind your business. Be sincere. Be respectful.
State expectations in positive terms.	Be safe. Be respectful. Be responsible.	Don't fight. Don't bring drugs or weapons on school property. Don't be mean.
Keep the expectations brief and simple.	Be there and be ready.	Be fully prepared and on time when you arrive at your location.
Make sure expectations can easily translate to concrete behaviors.	Follow directions. Accept responsibility. Respect ourselves and others.	Be eager, diverse, and steadfast.

Create Rules for Specific Events Using an Events-Expectations Matrix

After a teacher creates expectations, he or she can use them to develop rules for specific events within the classroom. As previously explained, expectations are purposefully broadly defined (for example, "Be respectful"), whereas rules are more concrete and narrowly defined (for example, "Raise your hand before speaking"). Expectations and rules go hand in hand—rules are applications of expectations to specific situations. Rules vary depending on context, with new rules emerging from the same expectation in different school settings. For example, the expectation "Be respectful" applies differently during teacher-led instruction (which may include the rule "Raise your hand to speak") than it does during a transition period in the hallway (which might include the rule "Walk quietly so as to not disturb others"). Before creating rules, therefore, teachers must identify the main events—tasks, activities, and routines—that take place during the day in a school or classroom.

To identify the events for which specific rules will be needed, first list the major activities and tasks that occur during a typical day, prioritizing those that students spend the most time doing or that are the most essential to ensure that activities and transitions run smoothly. Such events might include teacher-led instruction, small-group work, testing, arriving in the morning, leaving at the end of the day, transition time between class periods, lining up at the door, lunchtime, taking attendance, and so on. Next, combine items on the list into categories of related events. For example, teachers might consolidate silent reading, independent mathematics practice, and journal writing into a single event called independent work time.

Once a teacher has identified classroom events, he or she can use the expectations to construct an events-expectations matrix to develop rules for the classroom (Colvin, 2007; George, Kincaid, & Pollard-Sage, 2009; Netzel & Eber, 2003; Simonsen, Sugai, & Negron, 2008). The matrix outlines how each expectation manifests differently depending on the event, and it is used as both a reference point and teaching tool throughout the school year. Teachers can use an events-expectations matrix to both create rules and clarify to students how each expectation translates into rules for each classroom event. It states what each expectation looks like in a given setting. As the teacher creates a matrix, it is common to have similar rules across events and expectations. For example, "Keep your hands and feet to yourself" can apply to more than one expectation and event. Table 2.3 displays a sample events-expectations matrix for an elementary school classroom.

Table 2.3: Sample Events-Expectations Matrix for an Elementary School Classroom

Expectations	Rules				
	Morning Routine	**Lining Up**	**Lunchtime**	**Group Work**	**Seat Work**
Be Safe	• Hang up your coat and backpack. • Walk in the hallways. • Keep your hands to yourself.	• Walk. • Push your chair in after getting out of your seat. • Keep your hands to yourself.	• Sit pretzel-legged. • Eat your own food.	• Keep your hands to yourself. • Use materials appropriately. • Stay in your area.	• Use materials appropriately. • Stay in your seat.
Be Respectful	• Give others space.	• Give others space. • Use an inside voice.	• Use good manners.	• Follow directions. • Allow others to share.	• Follow directions. • Raise your hand.
Be Responsible	• Indicate on the board whether you brought a lunch or will buy lunch.	• Wait to be called.	• Throw trash away. • Recycle.	• Participate. • Stay on task.	• Stay on task. • Do your own work.

Source: Adapted from George et al., 2009.

As shown in table 2.3, each cell contains rules that guide students to behave according to expectations in each event. It is important to note that in addition to varying based on events and expectations, rules will also vary depending on the age of students. For instance, elementary school teachers may use a matrix that reflects the fact that students primarily stay in the same classroom throughout the day or do not move from room to room frequently. Table 2.4 (page 22) is an example of a matrix for a secondary setting. Teachers may decide to include a column containing rules that transcend different contexts or events, and therefore apply to students all the time. Within the Classroom column are rules that apply to all events and contexts, such as "Use appropriate language" or "Keep your hands and feet to yourself." It is more common to have such a column for older students, as they do not necessarily need such explicit rules for every event as younger students do (Gable et al., 2009). Table 2.4 also includes a row labeled Teacher Responsibilities, which lists the behaviors that teachers must perform to help students successfully follow the rules in each event. For example, a teacher may need to monitor the hallways and classroom entrance to help students succeed during a morning routine.

Table 2.4: Sample Events-Expectations Matrix for a Secondary School Classroom

Expectations	Events			
	Classroom	**Independent Work**	**Group Work and Discussion**	**End of Class and After School**
Respect Self	• Sit in your assigned seat before the bell rings. • Dress appropriately. • Self-monitor behavior.	• Keep all chair legs on the floor. • Complete your own work.	• Contribute to the work. • Participate. • Stay on task.	• Arrive on time for activities and clubs. • Carry your school I.D. everywhere. • Dress appropriately.
Respect Others	• Give people personal space. • Say positive things.	• Work quietly. • Share materials. • Raise your hand to share.	• Allow others to share. • Use active listening. • Stay on topic. • Cooperate with others.	• Give people personal space. • Hold the door for others.
Respect Learning	• Bring required materials. • Keep your cell phone stored out of sight. • Work quietly.	• Complete your own work. • Use materials appropriately.	• Contribute to the project or task. • Allow others to share.	• Leave the space clean and tidy. • Write down homework.
Teacher Responsibilities	• Use precorrection and remind students of expectations throughout the day. • Be sure to praise.	• Provide clear directions. • Monitor and praise students. • Offer options for students who complete work early.	• Move around the room, scan, and interact with students.	• Stand by the entrance and say goodbye to students.

Source: Adapted from Sheinhorn, 2008.

Teachers can use the "Classroom Matrix Template" (page 34) to create an events-expectations matrix for their own classrooms.

To help identify the specific rules for each event and complete the matrix, teachers can work backwards. First, identify the desired outcome for an event. Then, imagine the potential errors or undesired outcomes. Finally, write rules to prevent the errors and lead students to the desired outcome. To complete this process, teachers can use an outcome-errors chart such as the one in table 2.5. As shown, this strategy involves listing classroom events, the desired outcome for each, mistakes that students may make, and the corresponding rules for each event. Once the rules are listed, they can be transferred to the matrix under the appropriate expectation. This method is helpful because envisioning the goal for each event can make identifying the rules easier and ensure that the rules are comprehensive.

Table 2.5: Sample Outcome-Errors Chart for Creating Rules

Event	Desired Outcome	Potential Errors	Rules
Independent Seat Work	Students work quietly and complete their work.	• Talking to peers • Not asking for help if they get stuck	• Work quietly. • Raise your hand to ask for help. • Complete work neatly. • Clean up your area when you are done.
Leaving the Classroom	Students clean up their area and leave the classroom quickly, quietly, and without disruption.	• Talking to peers • Leaving a mess • Disrupting others in classroom or other classes	• Clean up materials. • Respect personal space. • Allow the person in front of you to go first.
Free Academic Time	Students work quietly on preferred tasks without disrupting others.	• Distracting others • Not knowing what to work on • Talking, blurting out	• Work quietly and respect others' work time. • Look at your list of to-do items to identify tasks to do. • Raise your hand if you need help.

The guidelines for writing rules are somewhat similar to the guidelines for writing expectations. For one, rules should apply to all students, be positively stated, and be expressed in simple language. Unlike expectations, however, rules should be very explicit. They should clarify what an expectation specifically looks and sounds like during a given classroom event. Focus on the most important and relevant rules for success in a given context. Avoid a long, exhaustive list of every possible rule. Finally, only include rules that govern likely behaviors involved in a particular situation. For instance, students who are learning the routine for lining up at the classroom door will probably not need—at that time—rules about disposing of trash or completing homework on time.

Actively Teach Expectations and Rules

After a teacher defines classroom expectations and rules, he or she can begin teaching them to students. This instruction should go beyond posting a list of classroom rules. Instead, students should receive direct instruction in how to behave, just as they receive direct instruction in academic content.

To do this, teachers design and execute lessons on expectations. These lessons can be taught in one time period or broken up across several days, depending on the age of students and the personal preference of the teacher. In a study by Shannon Langland, Teri Lewis-Palmer, and George Sugai (1998), two middle school teachers developed lesson plans for two expectations ("Showing respect to staff" and "Showing respect to peers"). They taught the lessons over the course of three days, devoting the first fifteen minutes of each class to the lesson. During these three days, students learned the definition of respect, studied examples and nonexamples of respect, and then engaged in activities that extended their learning (such as role-playing, generating additional examples, and so on). Following the lessons, the teachers spent time correcting and reminding students of respectful behavior, as well as providing praise when they noticed students being respectful. The rate of disrespectful behavior in class dropped by more than 60 percent (from 0.11 instances per minute to 0.04 instances per minute). Based on the research by Langland and her colleagues (1998), we recommend that expectation lessons include the following components:

- Definition and rationale for the expectation
- Examples and nonexamples
- Practice activities
- Prompting activities
- Follow-up and monitoring

A teacher might devote a portion of the day to teaching expectations. He or she could begin by introducing the definition and rationale for each expectation to students. Next, the teacher would take students to each routine setting and discuss examples and nonexamples of the expectations in each setting. To practice expectations in the group work setting, the teacher leads students in acting out what the expectations could look like in that setting. The teacher explains that she will use a specific word or phrase to prompt the students to follow the expectation in the future. To follow up, students return to their desks to draw and write about how to follow the expectations. Tables 2.6 and 2.7 (pages 24–26) provide sample lesson plans for teaching expectations.

Table 2.6: Sample Lesson Plan for Teaching the Expectation "Be Respectful"

Step	Teacher Actions	Example
Step 1: Expectation	Identify the expected behavior.	Be respectful.
Step 2: Rationale	Provide a rationale for teaching the expectation.	It is important for us to respect each other because we all have a right to feel safe and valued. While we are each individuals, together we are one class. Being respectful to each other will create a safe, open, and collaborative classroom.
Step 3: Examples	Define a range of examples.	When the teacher is explaining the next activity to the class, you can show respect by listening quietly with your hands in your lap and your eyes on the teacher. During group work, a student who you don't usually work with asks to join your group. You can show respect by letting him or her join the group.
	Define nonexamples.	During carpet time, the teacher asks you to come to the circle for a story. You stay at the computer looking at animal pictures. While lining up for lunch, you cut in front of other students to get through the line sooner.

Step	Teacher Actions	Example
Step 4: Practice	Use activities to practice the expectation.	The teacher has students draw pictures of themselves showing respect in various settings and routines (on their own, with family, during recess, and so on). The teacher has students perform skits about a time someone treated them with respect.
Step 5: Prompting	List methods to prompt and remind students of the expectation.	The teacher posts the expectations in the classroom where everyone can see them. The teacher reminds students of the expectations before events that are conducive to problem behaviors (such as transitions).
Step 6: Monitor	Describe how to monitor student progress relative to the expectation.	The teacher has the students color in a class bar graph for every Caught Being Good ticket they receive. When the bar graph is full, the class earns a reward. The teacher tracks office referrals for the class to identify which behaviors to reteach.

Source: Adapted from Langland et al., 1998.

Table 2.7: Example Lesson Plan for Teaching the Expectation "Act With Integrity"

Step	Teacher Actions	Example
Step 1: Expectation	Identify the expected behavior.	Act with integrity.
Step 2: Rationale	Provide a rationale for teaching the expectation.	It is important for us to have integrity because we want to be trusted when we speak and we want to trust others when they speak.
Step 3: Examples	Define a range of examples.	While working on a research project, you clearly cite references and paraphrase quotations in your own words. On your way out of the classroom, you accidentally knock a paperweight off the teacher's desk. When the teacher hears the commotion, you explain that you accidentally broke the paperweight.
	Define nonexamples.	In the computer lab, you check your social media page instead of working on your assignment. You hear a rumor about another student and then send text messages to your friends to share the rumor.
Step 4: Practice	Use activities to practice the expectation.	Have students work in groups to create a poem, song, or rap about integrity. Have students write a letter to stores, shops, and government representatives about showing integrity in the community.

Continued on next page →

Step	Teacher Actions	Example
Step 5: Prompting	List methods to prompt and remind students of the expectation.	Post the expectations in the classroom where everyone can see them. Reference them prior to beginning certain activities. Have students verbally share the expectations before they are released for the next class or activity.
Step 6: Monitor	Describe how to monitor student progress relative to the expectation.	Have students track the number of Caught Being Good tickets they earn in their planners. Display the weekly or quarterly totals in the classroom. Use the public display to track the extent to which students are demonstrating the expectations.

Source: Adapted from Langland et al., 1998.

The following sections elucidate each of the elements from Langland and her colleagues' (1998) research and provide strategies and resources to support their use. Use "Lesson Plan Template for Teaching Expectations" (page 35) to create lesson plans for teaching expectations that incorporate these strategies.

Definition and Rationale

Begin a lesson on a behavioral expectation by defining it. Simply state it and explain what it means to students. Next, provide a rationale to justify the expectation to students and help them understand how it can benefit them. For example, consider the expectation "Be responsible." Teachers might first facilitate a class discussion about the meaning of responsibility, and then refer to students' futures to provide rationale for this expectation (for example, "Responsibility is important now because we are learning to be productive, lifelong learners"). Social- or group-based rationales are also effective (for example, "We are safe because it makes it easier for everyone to learn"). Table 2.8 presents other examples of rationales for various expectations.

Some teachers may wish to clarify the relevance of their expectations or rules by providing definitions and rationales in the context of an event. In this case, students physically travel to the setting in which the event takes place or perform a routine associated with the event while the teacher explains the rationale for the expectation. Alternatively, teachers can arrange a station rotation activity to teach expectations. This works particularly well for elementary school students. In this type of session, the teacher begins with an overview of the expectations, and then guides students as they rotate from event to event. At each station, students review and practice expectations for events (such as centers, seat work, carpet time, lineup, and entering and exiting the classroom).

Table 2.8: Sample Rationales for Expectations

Expectation	Rationale
Be Safe	We are safe to make sure everyone is free from harm.
Be Respectful	We are respectful because we want to treat others as we would like to be treated. Respect shows that we value our classmates and their opinions. Being respectful creates an open and collaborative classroom.

Expectation	Rationale
Be Responsible	Being responsible helps us work hard and learn what we need to know. Being responsible helps us reach our goals.
Have Integrity	It is important for us to have integrity because it shows we are honest and trustworthy. We want to be trusted when we say something, and we want to trust others.
Be Prepared	Being prepared helps us start activities on time and get our work done. Being prepared helps us be successful.

Examples and Nonexamples

Once students can define and justify an expectation or rule, teachers should provide examples and nonexamples to clarify its range and boundaries. Examples should illustrate the expected behavior in different events, including scenarios that address common errors or problem behaviors. If students have trouble respecting personal space while lining up, for instance, give examples of positive and negative lineup behavior and ask students to compare them.

During the examples portion of the lesson, teachers may also invite students to act out the expectations in a role-play scenario. Asking students to act out examples allows the teacher to provide feedback, coaching, and correction. Observe as students demonstrate the behavior to ensure that it meets the expectation. If a student makes a mistake, correct the behavior and offer the student another chance to demonstrate it properly. Students do not need to act out nonexamples for expectations—they may end up learning negative behaviors. Instead, focus on demonstrating different ways of adhering to expectations.

Practice Activities

At this point in the lesson, students should have a clear idea of what the expectation or rule stipulates, as well as which types of behaviors are acceptable. When this is the case, students are ready to engage in practice activities that deepen their knowledge of expectations and rules. Practice is an important part of teaching expectations because many students will need several repetitions to learn a behavioral skill, particularly if the skill is completely new to them (Anhalt et al., 1998; Lewis et al., 2004; Stormont et al., 2007). The practice portion of the lesson plan also extends the learning and provides students an opportunity to ingrain the expectation into their daily routine. Regular practice and review of expectations can help teachers maintain low levels of disruptive and unwanted behavior (Taylor-Greene et al., 1997). To practice expectations and rules with students, teachers can engage the class in a variety of activities. Table 2.9 lists several examples of practice activities.

Table 2.9: Activities for Practicing Expectations and Rules

Activity	Description
Role Plays	Students role-play the expectations with each other in various scenarios.
Stories	Students write or read stories in which characters follow the expectations.

Continued on next page →

Activity	Description
Essays and Letters	Students write essays or letters to parents or community members about how the class follows the expectations.
Skits	Small groups of students create skits illustrating the importance of different expectations.
Songs, Raps, and Poems	Students write and perform songs, raps, or poems about the expectations.
Drawings and Posters	Students draw pictures or make posters depicting people following the expectations.
Discussions	Students answer questions and discuss hypothetical scenarios involving the expectations.

Prompts

After teaching and practicing an expectation or rule with students, explain that you will use prompts to offer them occasional reminders to follow it. *Prompts* are verbal statements, gestures, models, visual cues, or physical movements that remind students to perform a desired behavior (Wolery et al., 1988). Table 2.10 displays examples for each type of prompt.

Table 2.10: Prompts to Use

Type of Prompt	Examples
Verbal Statements	Prior to a silent reading activity, a teacher points out that students were noisy the previous day, which did not meet the expectations for silent reading time. She reminds them of the expectation to be respectful and sets a goal for them.
	At the beginning of each class period, a teacher asks a few students to share how they followed expectations the day before.
	Before releasing his class for recess, a teacher asks students to watch for and praise classmates who are following the expectations.
Gestures	A teacher holds a finger over her mouth to tell students to use an indoor voice when coming in from recess.
Models	A teacher models the correct way to turn in homework by quietly getting up from his seat, walking to the homework basket, and gently placing his paper atop the stack.
Visual Cues	The expectations are posted at the front of the classroom.
	Every morning, a teacher places a small visual reminder to follow expectations—such as a small figurine of the school's mascot—on a different student's desk.
Physical Movements	A teacher gently touches a student's shoulder to indicate where to stand when lining up.
	A teacher moves a student's seat to help him pay attention during class time.

Source: Adapted from Wolery et al., 1988.

Teachers should explain and demonstrate the prompt(s) they will use for various expectations so that students will be able to recognize and respond appropriately when the prompts are used in context.

Follow-Up and Monitoring

Following the teaching of expectations, teachers will want to monitor students' behavior to ensure that they are displaying the expectations. *Monitoring* is the process of collecting data on students' behavior and evaluating whether teaching the expectations yielded a positive behavior change. For example, a teacher might keep track of how often the class lines up safely and efficiently versus how often students become distracted or rowdy during that event.

It is also important that students do not forget the expectations after the initial lesson. Students will need direct reminders to follow them, but teachers also can and should embed the expectations within various lessons. This can facilitate generalization of the skills beyond the classroom, and it can help students view the expectations as an active part of the classroom's culture. For example, lessons on respect can be embedded in units on novels and stories that the class reads by asking students to reflect upon how the characters showed (or did not show) respect. If an expectation is empathy or compassion, students can write essays on how historical figures showed compassion or empathy. Students can develop songs, videos, and skits on the expectations as part of a fine arts class (for example, music, art, computer, or graphic design class; Florida's Positive Behavior Support Project, n.d.).

Even when students have followed classroom rules and expectations for weeks, they may gradually adhere to rules and expectations less as the school year progresses. Students may even forget about certain ones, especially during particular times of the year. For instance, behavior issues tend to spike before or after a vacation from school (such as a long weekend or holiday break; Alberto & Troutman, 2013; Taylor-Greene et al., 1997). To proactively reduce behavior issues in advance of these events, teachers can briefly review the expectations in the form of booster sessions. A *booster session* is a brief review of the expectations and can be conducted with the whole class, a small group, or an individual student. As with academic subjects, the amount of review that each student needs varies. Some students need only minimal instruction in expectations (that is, once or twice at the beginning of the year), whereas others may need monthly, weekly, or daily mini-lessons and reminders. Still others may only need brief reviews following each weekend or break from school. Teachers can tailor instruction on expectations to suit the individual needs of each student. To decide when and where students need review of expectations and rules, teachers can monitor students' behavior and use the data to inform decisions.

Teachers can also expand and deepen students' understanding of the expectations, particularly for older students. During monthly or weekly *focus lessons*, break down an expectation into more discrete skills. For example, if a teacher expects students to be respectful, he might decide to teach a different trait related to respect each month (such as cooperation, empathy, ownership, and so on). During the focus lesson, he defines the trait and then engages students in activities or events related to that trait. After a few months, the focus shifts to a new expectation and the teacher uses focus lessons to introduce new traits related to that expectation.

One issue related to classroom expectations and rules arises when new students arrive in the middle of the year. In order to get a new student up to speed, teachers can certainly set aside time for a one-on-one conversation. However, this may not be the most efficient method. Alternatively, designate another student in the class to introduce and teach the class expectations to the new student, keeping in mind that the student you choose must be very familiar with the expectations. Provide a worksheet or checklist to both students to ensure that all necessary aspects of the expectations are covered. Another option involves the use of an expectations "passport," a small booklet that contains a page for each classroom event. Whenever the new student "visits" a new event, the veteran student explains the expectations and rules in that setting. The new student receives a stamp or signature from the veteran student upon learning the expectations. The new student then "travels" to another activity and the process repeats. This option creates a document for the new student that the teacher can use to track the expectations the new student has learned (Florida's Positive Behavior Support Project, n.d.).

Summary

This chapter provided an overview of identifying and teaching classroom expectations, which are foundational parts of classroom management. Teachers should identify three to five broad expectations that are proactively taught to students. These expectations are translated into specific, concrete rules for various events and listed in a classroom matrix. Both expectations and rules are positively worded and action oriented. Once expectations and rules are defined for the classroom, the next step is to identify procedures for the various tasks within the classroom. The next chapter discusses how to teach procedures to students, and discusses considerations for organizing the classroom to promote structure.

Chapter 2: Comprehension Questions

1. What are the similarities and differences between expectations and rules?

2. Describe two methods for identifying expectations. What are the pros and cons of each?

3. Why would a teacher want to provide a rationale for an expectation when teaching it to students?

4. What are some ways the expectations can be reviewed throughout the school year?

Conducting Observations to Identify Expectations

Use this form to collect data for identifying expectations. To conduct the observation, observe the class for five to ten minutes at several points in time, marking a tally for each instance of a behavior. The same form can be used across several observations. After conducting several observations, the data can be analyzed to help identify needed expectations.

The five steps are:

1. Determine the behaviors to observe and operationally define each behavior. Some typical behaviors to watch for are listed on the form, but other behaviors can be added if needed.

2. Arrange opportunities for observers to watch your classroom at various times and on different days. This does not have to be formal; observers can simply come into the classroom to observe at their convenience.

3. After several observations have been conducted and sufficient data have been gathered, tally the occurrences of each behavior.

4. Analyze the frequencies to find the most common behaviors that students display. It is best to organize this information in a bar chart.

5. Create expectations that address the most problematic behaviors.

page 1 of 2

Observation Date/Time	Type of Problematic Behavior											
	Defiance	Disrespect to Teacher	Disrespect to Peer	Disruption	Physical Contact	Physical Aggression	Inappropriate Language	Property Misuse	Tardiness	Technology Violation	Other: _____	Other: _____
Totals:												

page 2 of 2

Classroom Matrix Template

Expectations	Rules				
	Event: _____	Event: _____	Event: _____	Event: _____	Event: _____

Lesson Plan Template for Teaching Expectations

Step	Teacher Actions	Description of Plan
Step 1: Expectation	Identify the expected behavior.	
Step 2: Rationale	Provide a rationale for teaching the expectation.	
Step 3: Examples	Define a range of examples.	
	Define nonexamples.	
Step 4: Practice	Use activities to practice the expectation.	
Step 5: Prompting	List methods to prompt and remind students of the expectation.	
Step 6: Monitor	Describe how to monitor student progress relative to the expectation.	

Source: Adapted from Langland, S., Lewis-Palmer, T., & Sugai, G. (1998). Teaching respect in the classroom: An instructional approach. *Journal of Behavioral Education, 8,* 245–262.

Chapter 3

ESTABLISHING PROCEDURES AND STRUCTURE

A second component of effective classroom management involves establishing classroom procedures and structure. As previously explained, students engage in a number of events throughout the school day (such as completing independent seat work, turning in homework, and so on). In order to succeed in these events, students benefit from a certain degree of structure. *Structure* refers to the amount of predictability within the classroom, including established procedures for specific activities. For example, students should understand how to turn in homework when it is due or ask for help during seat work. Clear structure in classrooms is associated with fewer problem behaviors and higher academic results (Marzano, 2003; Stronge et al., 2011; Walker, Ramsey, & Gresham, 2003), and structure also provides students with clear parameters as to how to succeed within the classroom (Darch & Kame'enui, 2003; Marzano, 2003).

Teachers can take three steps to establish procedures and structure in their classrooms.

1. Organize the physical layout of the classroom to minimize behavior issues.

2. Generate a list of classroom procedures with goals and steps.

3. Teach the procedures using a model, lead, test format.

The following sections describe each of these steps in detail.

Organize the Classroom

The first way for teachers to create a structured classroom environment is to ensure that the classroom is physically designed to curtail problem behavior. Strategically organize desks and materials to avoid creating areas in the classroom that provoke or encourage behavior issues. A well-organized classroom can reduce the number of antecedents that trigger problematic behavior (Bettenhausen, 1998; Evertson & Emmer, 2013; Trussell, 2008).

Generally speaking, effective classroom layouts allow people to move around the classroom with ample space and without disturbing others. For one, place frequently used materials—such as the pencil sharpener or waste basket—in an easily accessible location away from students' desks to avoid distraction. Also, organize classroom furniture carefully to keep high-traffic areas free of congestion. Robert Trussell (2008) called this the *bump factor* of a classroom, or the likelihood of students running into each other's desks or materials. Finally, design the classroom to support functions of teaching. Make sure all students can see the teacher—as well as the projector screen, boards, and whole-class displays—and that the teacher can see all students. Arrange desks differently based on the structure of the class, using independent seats to facilitate engagement during direct instruction or grouped seating to encourage discussion and cooperative learning.

Figure 3.1 depicts an example of a classroom layout that has the potential to produce some problematic behaviors.

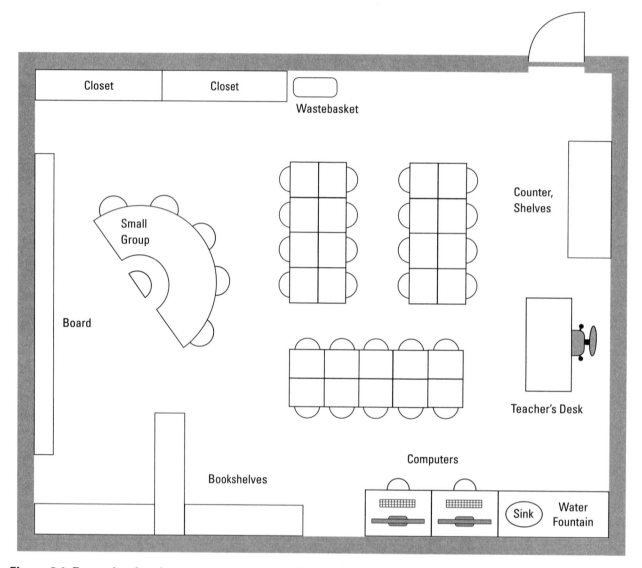

Figure 3.1: Example of a classroom arrangement that enables problematic behavior.

Source: Adapted from Evertson & Emmer, 2013.

As shown in figure 3.1, there are a few issues with the layout. First, the bookshelves in the bottom left corner of the room create a place where students can sit out of the teacher's sight. Second, some students are seated such that they have their backs to the board. Third, the high-traffic area for the computers, sink, and water fountain are in close proximity to students' desks, creating opportunities for traffic jams and disruption. Figure 3.2, on the other hand, illustrates an effective classroom layout.

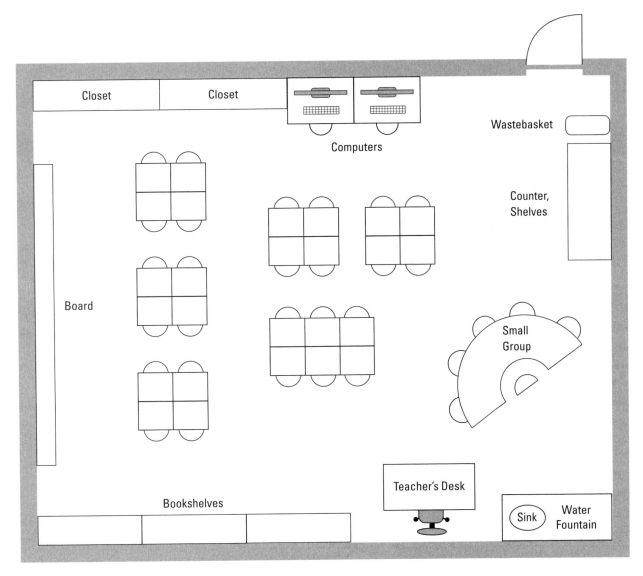

Figure 3.2: Example of effective classroom arrangement.

Source: Adapted from Evertson & Emmer, 2013.

This layout provides a setting less likely to create problem behavior. As shown in figure 3.2, the small group table is away from students' desks, and the teacher can sit with the small group and still see all of the students. All students can easily see the board while seated at their desks, and high-traffic areas are away from work areas and not near students' desks. "Classroom Layout Checklist" (page 46) provides a checklist teachers can use to evaluate their classroom layout.

A final consideration when organizing the classroom is the creation and use of a schedule. The schedule lets students know what to expect in terms of the order of events each day. The predictability that clear schedules add to the classroom increases students' sense of security. Students' familiarity with schedules is also associated with higher engagement and fewer behavior problems (Ostrosky, Jung, Hemmeter, & Thomas, 2008). When developing a schedule of events, keep in mind the following guidelines.

- Schedule less desirable tasks before highly desirable tasks—for example, independent work before group work, or difficult academic tasks prior to a relaxing activity or recess.

- Balance the energy level between tasks—for example, follow a high-energy task with a lower-energy task to moderate students' energy levels.

- Try to break longer instructional periods into smaller, more manageable segments.

- Visually display the schedule and call attention to it as a way to help students manage their time.

- Alert students to any changes in the schedule well before the change occurs—for example, tell students at the beginning of the day if there are changes to the afternoon schedule.

The physical and temporal organization of the classroom forms an essential foundation for a well-structured class.

List Procedures, Goals, and Steps

Procedures are processes that students carry out to successfully complete classroom events. Teachers might develop procedures for requesting help during independent seat work, getting permission to use the restroom, turning in homework, and so on. Procedures ensure that the classroom operates smoothly. A procedure outlines a series of steps students take in order to manage a task on their own, with little to no teacher guidance. For example, students need a procedure for going to the restroom. This procedure may consist of a few steps:

1. Look to see if the pass is available. If it is not, wait until the student with it returns.

2. When the pass is available, leave your seat and get the pass.

3. Sign out on the sheet by the pass. Be sure to write your name and the time you are leaving.

4. Go quickly and quietly to the restroom.

5. Return to class.

6. Put the pass back in its place, and write the time you are back on the sheet.

Once students learn a procedure, they should practice it several times until they no longer need instruction and guidance from a teacher. Teachers can design two categories of procedures: (1) procedures for classroom events, and (2) procedures for transitions.

Procedures for Classroom Events

Teachers can begin creating procedures for their classrooms by brainstorming a list of routine tasks that students will have to perform in the classroom. Table 3.1 provides some examples of classroom events that might require procedures.

Table 3.1: Examples of Elementary and Secondary School Procedures

Elementary Examples	Secondary Examples
Entering the classroom	Completing bell work
Lining up	Turning in homework
Asking to use the restroom	Asking to use the restroom

Elementary Examples	Secondary Examples
Turning in homework folders	Asking for help
Transitioning to a new activity	Using the computer

Whereas teaching expectations involves general lessons that encompass several different classroom events, teachers should focus on one event at a time when teaching procedures. After generating a list of events that require procedures, identify a goal or desired outcome for each one. Table 3.2 displays a list of sample procedures and corresponding goals.

Table 3.2: Classroom Procedures and Corresponding Goals

Procedure	Goal (Desired Outcome)
Lining up	To quickly create a line of quiet students at the classroom door
Entering the classroom	To enter the classroom quietly without causing disruption
Turning in homework	To turn in homework quickly and in an organized manner
Asking to use the restroom	To obtain permission for using the restroom in a nondisruptive manner
Obtaining help from the teacher	To seek needed help from the teacher in a respectful manner without disrupting the whole class

Finally, create a series of steps students can take to achieve the specified goal for each procedure. Conduct a task analysis for each procedure that ends with the student achieving the goal. A *task analysis* is the process of breaking down a task into a series of small steps (Wolery et al., 1988). For example, consider a procedure for using the computer. In this case, the goal is for students to use the computer appropriately and within the allotted time. Steps for this procedure may include the following:

1. When it is your turn, sit at the computer (and push the power button if the computer is off).

2. Write your name and the time on the login sheet.

3. Set the timer for ten minutes.

4. Open and play one of the educational games.

5. When the timer goes off, stop playing the game and exit the program.

6. Write down the time you stopped on the login sheet.

7. Return to your desk so someone else may have a turn.

"Template for Creating Procedures" (page 47) can guide teachers as they devise a list of procedures, goals, and steps. When creating this list, keep in mind that certain events or lesson segments can be especially conducive to problematic behavior when left unregulated. To prevent a smooth-running lesson from unraveling, pay particular attention to creating procedures for transitions.

Procedures for Transitions

A *transition* is a specific type of procedure that refers to "a shift or change from one activity to another" (Wolery et al., 1988, p. 199). Transitions include the time between two activities, during which students finish one task and then organize and prepare for the next one (Buck, 1999; Wolery et al., 1988; Yarbrough, Skinner, Lee, & Lemmons, 2004). Transitions can be simple and brief (such as closing and storing a reading book and then opening a math book) or complex and involved (such as moving from one classroom to another or packing up at the end of the day). If teachers do not establish efficient and quick transition procedures, transitions can invite problematic behavior. Students who do not know specific steps for appropriately ending one activity and beginning another are more prone to leave materials out, disrupt one another, and arrive at a new activity unprepared (Buck, 1999). Given that unclear, lengthy, or disorganized transition times can set up problem behavior, it is important that teachers facilitate efficient transitions.

Consider the work of Jamie Yarbrough and her colleagues (2004), which proposed an organized method for ensuring quick transitions. The researchers worked with a second-grade teacher whose class engaged in disruptive behavior (such as jumping, yelling, running, dancing, and pushing). Disruptions were most severe when students returned to the classroom after lunchtime, which delayed the start of the next activity. In response, Yarbrough and her colleagues (2004) implemented what they called the Timely Transitions Game (TTG). The TTG involved group contingencies (consequences applied based on group behavior) and public displays of progress (evidence of improvement—or lack thereof—that everyone can see) to encourage behavioral change. First, they told students that if they were ready for class within a certain time limit after lunch, they would earn a popcorn party. When the first student entered the classroom after lunch, the teacher started a timer. When every student was seated quietly at his or her desk, the teacher stopped the timer. Each day, the teacher reminded the students of the procedure before they left for lunch, and after lunch she stood by the doorway and reminded them of the procedure as they entered the room. When the timer stopped, the teacher wrote the total transition time for the day on the board. At the end of the day, the teacher chose randomly from a basket containing thirteen cards. Written on each card was a different amount of time. The times ranged from forty seconds to one hundred seconds. Whenever the students transitioned from lunch back to class in less time than was displayed on the card, the teacher wrote a letter on the board. When the letters spelled out P-A-R-T-Y, they earned a party the next day. Before the TTG was implemented, the class had an average transition time of over three minutes after lunch. After twenty-seven days of the TTG, the students' transition time was less than fifty seconds. More importantly, the teacher reported that she was no longer emotionally exhausted from prompting and pestering the students to settle down after lunch. The TTG has also been used effectively with older students (Campbell & Skinner, 2004). Although not all transitions will require the elements that Yarbrough and her colleagues used (for example, explicit timing, group contingency, public displays of progress), these elements can be used to teach students to transition quickly and smoothly.

The preceding example addresses one specific transition period. However, transitions occur frequently throughout the day. Therefore, a teacher might also decide to establish a general transition procedure for students that applies to many different types of transitions. A general transition procedure might include the following steps.

1. On the teacher's signal, students put away materials and supplies.

2. Students move quickly and quietly to the next activity, keeping their hands and feet to themselves.

3. Students take out their materials and supplies for the next activity, if applicable (some activities may require students to simply return to their desks and wait for more directions).

4. Students fold their hands in their laps and look at the teacher to indicate that they are ready to begin.

As indicated in step 1, teachers can establish signals to help them in creating organized transitions. A *signal* is any visual or auditory prompt that tells students to stop what they are doing and pay attention to the teacher. From there, teachers can ensure that students hear the directions (Alberto & Troutman, 2013; Wolery et al., 1988). Some teachers prefer auditory signals because they reach students whose eyes are not on the teacher; others prefer visual signals because they keep the classroom quiet. Examples of signals include the following.

- The teacher says, "Class?" and students stop, look at the teacher, and respond with an elongated "Yes?"

- The teacher turns the lights out and students stop and look at the teacher for direction.

- The teacher rings a chime to indicate a transition is coming, and then rings a slightly different chime to tell students to transition to the next activity.

No matter which signal you use, be sure to directly teach it to students so that they understand what it means when it occurs. Use the signal for only one purpose so as not to confuse the class. Because signals are meant to tell students to immediately respond and begin performing the activity or routine the signal indicates, they need lots of practice and reinforcement.

In addition to signals, teachers can utilize a number of other strategies to enhance their transitions. Refer to the following guidelines when designing transition procedures.

- Provide two minutes of advance notice before a transition to allow students to wind down from an activity.

- Practice transitions until they are quick and efficient, taking just a few minutes to complete.

- Take care to avoid giving conflicting directions, changing tasks abruptly, returning to an old activity after starting a new one, or providing incorrect information (such as instructing students to take out the wrong textbook).

- Provide activities for students to do while waiting for others to complete a transition. For example, classroom stations allow students to move from one area of the classroom to the next as they complete activities, leading to more efficient transitions and higher engagement (Wolery et al., 1988).

- Play background music during a transition to give students a sense of when the transition should end. The transition can be timed and students can be given countdowns to ensure they move quickly.

- As described previously, reinforcement can be provided based on how long (or short) transitions take, especially if transitions have become disruptive or problematic. This might include praise, tangible rewards, group contingency, public displays of progress, and so on.

Once teachers have created a list of procedures and identified goals and steps for each one, they can begin introducing procedures to students.

Model, Lead, and Test Procedures

Education researchers and theorists have devised a variety of different methods and terminology for teaching procedures. Most of these approaches have a few key steps in common. Typically, teachers are encouraged to explicitly teach and model the procedure and then give students a chance to practice it. For example, Wong and Wong (2009) described an "explain, rehearse, reinforce" (p. 177) approach to establishing procedures. Similarly, Lee Canter's (2010) assertive discipline approach included setting clear expectations, verbally acknowledging positive behaviors (what Canter calls "behavioral narration" [p. 63]), and correcting negative behaviors. PBIS researchers have also described a teaching process that involves modeling procedures (which they called *routines*) and having students practice them (George et al., 2009; Horner et al., 2005; Langland et al., 1998; Taylor-Greene et al., 1997). Douglas Fisher and Nancy Frey (2008) suggested that teachers use a similar approach to gradually transfer responsibility for behavior and learning to the students. Finally, Craig Darch and his colleagues (1998) encouraged teachers to directly teach behaviors and then offer students positive reinforcement for displaying them.

While each of these approaches incorporates its own unique strategies, they all involve the following three steps.

1. **Model:** The teacher explicitly shares and demonstrates the steps of the procedure.

2. **Lead:** Students demonstrate the steps of the procedure—with teacher guidance—until they can perform the steps without errors.

3. **Test:** Students practice the procedure independently without teacher guidance and receive feedback on their performance (the teacher provides praise when students successfully complete the procedure and provides corrective feedback—as well as a prompt to try the procedure again—when students are unsuccessful).

Teachers can use these three steps to guide the development of mini-lesson plans for procedures (see "Lesson Plan Template for Teaching Procedures" on page 48 for a lesson plan template). Lesson plans for procedures may be less extensive than those for expectations; still, they should always contain a few key components. First, choose which procedures to teach and how to teach them. Plan to spend the most time teaching and practicing procedures at the beginning of the year and then periodically review them throughout the year. Next, decide how to guide students as they demonstrate the procedures. Plan to practice procedures in context to help students experience them in realistic situations and lead students through each procedure, prompting them to complete every step in the process. Finally, decide how to test students' knowledge of procedures. This can be as simple as asking students to list the steps of the procedure, or requiring an active and accurate demonstration of the procedure. Provide praise or corrective feedback as appropriate.

Summary

This chapter provided considerations for teaching procedures to students and ways to organize the classroom. When students are unfamiliar with procedures or left to their own devices during a routine or activity, they may veer off task and become disruptive as a result. Creating structure and routine in the classroom is essential to classroom management because it ensures that students are prepared to navigate daily classroom activities efficiently. Effective classroom organization mitigates problem behavior; procedures create a predictable, secure environment for students and enable them to navigate common classroom events efficiently. Teachers can use a model, lead, test approach to teach procedures to students. Following the establishment of expectations, rules, and procedures for the classroom, teachers provide reinforcement and feedback to ensure students regularly follow those expectations, procedures, and rules. The next chapter discusses the use of reinforcement.

Chapter 3: Comprehension Questions

1. Why do students need to be taught procedures?

2. How can the physical layout of a classroom decrease problem behavior?

3. Why are transitions particularly important?

4. What is the general format for teaching procedures?

Classroom Layout Checklist

Use this checklist to ensure that the physical layout of the classroom minimizes triggers for problem behavior.

Feature	Yes	No
Are high-traffic areas (such as the pencil sharpener, sink, water fountain, and so on) free of congestion?		
Can all students be easily seen by the teacher and vice versa?		
Are frequently used materials easily accessible?		
Can all students see whole-class presentations (such as those on the projector and whiteboard) easily?		
Do students have ample room around their desks and seats?		
Are desks organized in a way that facilitates teaching (in circles for group work or individual seats for independent work, for example)?		
During small-group instruction, can the teacher still see all students?		
Does the layout accommodate students with special needs?		
Is there space available for students who need a quieter work environment or time to wind down?		

Template for Creating Procedures

List the goal of each procedure, as well as all of the steps students take to achieve the goal. Adjust the level of detail and the number of steps depending on the age of the students.

Procedure:		
Goal:		
Steps:	1	
	2	
	3	
	4	
	5	
	6	
	7	

Lesson Plan Template for Teaching Procedures

Procedure for: _____

Step	Teacher Actions	Description of Plan
Step 1: Model	Explicitly share and demonstrate the steps of the procedure.	
Step 2: Lead	Guide students in practicing the procedure until they can perform it without errors.	
Step 3: Test	Have students practice the procedure independently; provide them with feedback.	

Chapter 4

REINFORCING EXPECTATIONS

Once teachers have established expectations, rules, and procedures in their classrooms, they can strengthen students' adherence to them by using reinforcement strategies. As discussed in chapter 1, reinforcement is something that occurs after a behavior that increases the likelihood that the behavior will occur again. Reinforcement strategies are important because they facilitate the learning and internalization of expectations. That is, reinforcement facilitates the development of intrinsic motivation for expectations. Within the classroom, teachers can use three types of reinforcement:

1. Behavior-specific praise

2. Rewards

3. Group contingencies

Teachers should include each type of reinforcement within their comprehensive reinforcement system. Here, we provide details about each type of reinforcement and suggest ways to design and implement a reinforcement system that allows teachers to effectively monitor and track students' adherence to expectations.

Behavior-Specific Praise

Teachers can use praise to reinforce appropriate behavior. When a teacher gives praise, he or she communicates that a student's behavior is appropriate or desired. Sometimes called *feedback* or *recognition*, it can be used to develop both academic and behavioral skills in students (Akin-Little, Eckert, Lovett, & Little, 2004; Brophy, 1981; Canter, 2010; Hattie & Timperley, 2007). Praise is important to master and use because it is an effective tool to guide students' behavior, and because it facilitates the transition from students' reliance on extrinsic motivation (such as tangible items or short-term rewards) to intrinsic motivation (such as natural and social reinforcement).

There are two types of praise: general praise and behavior-specific praise. *General praise* is vague and unattached to any particular behavior (Dweck, 2008; Reinke, Lewis-Palmer, & Martin, 2007). For example, a teacher might write "Good job!" or "Nice work!" on a student's essay. General praise statements are positively phrased; however, they do not tell a student exactly what he or she did that warranted praise. Although general praise can create a positive environment, it does not serve an instructional purpose and may not strengthen certain behaviors (Reinke, Herman, & Stormont, 2013; Reinke et al., 2007). *Behavior-specific praise*, by contrast, explicitly acknowledges a specific behavior (Lewis et al., 2004;

Sutherland, Wehby, & Copeland, 2000). For example, a teacher might say, "Thank you for coming into the classroom quietly and keeping your hands to yourself." Teachers using behavior-specific praise point out the desirable behavior the students are performing and offer acknowledgment that the behavior is correct or socially appropriate. Table 4.1 displays examples of behavior-specific and general praise.

Table 4.1: Examples of Behavior-Specific and General Praise

Behavior-Specific Praise	General Praise
John, thank you for raising your hand and waiting to be called on before answering.	Wow! You did such a good job!
Jill, you worked really hard and stayed focused on that assignment. I can tell you put a lot of work into it.	Jill, that is great! You're a hard worker!
Everyone contributed, and you all found a way to cooperate.	Super!
You're looking at me and following along. That tells me you're listening and you're ready to work.	Incredible! Yes!
I see you reviewed your work carefully and made sure it was neat before handing it in. That's very responsible.	You have such nice handwriting!
It's really respectful of you to hold the door for others as we come into the classroom.	You're so nice!

Behavior-specific praise provides more precise direction than general praise; it effectively reduces behavior issues and increases positive academic behaviors among students, such as staying on task, completing work, and engaging in content (Filcheck et al., 2004; Reinke et al., 2007; Sutherland et al., 2000). In a study of fifth-grade students with emotional and behavioral disorders, Kevin S. Sutherland, Joseph H. Wehby, and Susan R. Copeland (2000) found that when a teacher gave behavior-specific praise once every ten minutes, students stayed engaged in the lesson 48.7 percent of the time. By contrast, when the teacher gave behavior-specific praise once every two minutes, the students stayed engaged 85.6 percent of the time. Overall, specific praise for academic behavior is related to an increase in correct responses, work accuracy and production, and improved performance (Simonsen & Freeman, n.d.; Sutherland & Wehby, 2001).

Similarly, behavior-specific praise can help teachers improve students' social behavior. Behavior-specific praise for social behavior is associated with increases in student attention and on-task behavior (Gable et al., 2009; Simonsen & Freeman, n.d.; Sutherland et al., 2000). Additionally, studies have shown that behavior-specific praise is effective for improving academic and social behavior with both elementary (Anhalt et al., 1998; Chalk & Bizo, 2004; Stormont et al., 2007; Sutherland et al., 2000) and secondary students (Bohanon et al., 2006; Musti-Rao & Haydon, 2011).

It is important to note that the way a teacher delivers praise may vary depending on the student's unique needs. For example, some students might prefer to receive praise in front of their classmates (for example, when a teacher announces it in front of the whole class), whereas others may prefer private praise (Feldman, 2003; Gable et al., 2009). In general, younger students tend to prefer receiving more praise than do older students, and more students prefer private praise over public praise (Burnett, 2001; Gable et al., 2009). Ask your students which types of praise they prefer.

Students who require more frequent rates of praise in order to stay focused and meet expectations can use *self-recruitment of praise*, which involves the student seeking out a teacher or classmate and reporting his or her own positive behavior (Todd, Horner, & Sugai, 1999). For example, a mathematics teacher and student might agree on a self-recruitment arrangement in which the student comes up to the teacher's desk whenever he or she finishes a certain number of math problems. The teacher then provides praise and encourages the student to continue working. Student self-recruitment of praise dually benefits student and teacher; it affords occasional breaks for the student and reminds the teacher to offer praise, thus reducing the burden of constantly monitoring the amount of praise given to high-needs students.

The adjustment from general to behavior-specific praise may be awkward at first. Teachers who are just beginning to provide behavior-specific praise may begin by simply describing the student's behavior, a process that Lee Canter (2010) called *behavioral narration*. For example, a teacher might say something like, "Mary is sitting quietly. Jay has his eyes on me. I see Donovan is raising his hand to share." Teachers can also use the following general procedure for providing behavior-specific praise.

1. Notice a student behaving positively (for example, by holding the door for a classmate).

2. During or immediately after the behavior, approach the student and describe the behavior. ("You held the door open for your classmate.")

3. Make a value statement. ("That's very nice of you.")

4. Optionally, tie the behavior to an expectation, describing how it benefits others. ("That was very respectful—you helped us all exit the classroom quickly and without bumping into each other.")

5. Give the student a reward (such as a token, paper ticket, or some other short-term reward).

Notice that a tangible reward (if used) comes at the end of the interchange. This placement is intentional, as the focus of behavior-specific praise should be on the student's performing the behavior well and its natural consequences, rather than the administration of a reward. As rewards are phased out over time, the first four steps can still be used to provide behavior-specific praise.

In addition to these steps, teachers can observe a number of guidelines when implementing behavior-specific praise. First, convey warmth and genuine appreciation. Students can detect insincere praise (Gable et al., 2009; Partin, Robertson, Maggin, Oliver, & Wehby, 2010). To avoid seeming disingenuous to students, adhere to the if-then rule for giving praise: *if* students demonstrate correct behavior, *then* praise. Varying verbal praise statements can help make each one sound organic and candid. Teachers can use the following sentence stems to add variation to behavior-specific praise.

•   I see you _____ [describe behavior].

•   I know everyone appreciates it when you _____ [describe behavior].

•   Everyone, notice how _____ [student's name] is _____ [describe behavior]. That is demonstrating _____ [name an expectation].

Second, consider context and surroundings before offering praise. Fit praise into the flow of instruction to avoid disrupting or interrupting work. To this end, teachers might offer nonverbal praise (such as a thumbs-up or a smile) from across a room or during silent work time. Finally, pay attention to the amount of praise offered to students relative to the amount of correction and redirection you give. Researchers and educators refer to an optimal proportion of positive to corrective feedback as the *magic ratio.*

Wendy M. Reinke, Keith C. Herman, and Melissa Stormont (2013) explored how a teacher's ratio of positive feedback to corrective comments related to that teacher's self-efficacy and to rates of disruptive behavior in his or her classroom. They found that teachers with higher ratios of praise to redirects encountered fewer student disruptions in class. Additionally, teachers who had lower ratios reported feeling more emotionally exhausted and using harsher discipline strategies. The ideal rate (or magic ratio) of praise to negative comments is approximately five positive statements for every one negative statement (Flora, 2000; Kern, White, & Gresham, 2007; Reinke et al., 2013). The idea of the magic ratio for praise is not limited to the classroom. In his study on married couples, John Gottman (1994) analyzed the number of positive and negative statements made during the couples' interactions. With over 90 percent accuracy, Gottman used these ratios to predict whether couples would eventually divorce. Couples who used five positive statements to one negative statement were likely to stay married, whereas couples who used more negative statements than positive were typically headed for divorce. When Marcial Losada and Emily Heaphy (2004) examined the performance of management teams, they found that high-performing teams used about five positive statements ("That's a good idea!") for every one negative or disapproving statement ("That's ridiculous."). Medium-performing teams used about two positive statements for every negative one, and low-performing teams used slightly more negative than positive statements. Considering these statistics, teachers should strive to achieve a five-to-one positive-to-negative ratio when offering feedback to students.

Rewards

Rewards are an important and effective part of classroom management, though there has been some debate over their use. A number of researchers have questioned the usefulness of rewards for managing student behavior, wondering whether rewards teach students to be *extrinsically motivated* (driven to behave a certain way in order to receive a reward or evade a punishment) rather than *intrinsically motivated* (driven to behave a certain way because it is personally rewarding; for example, Deci, 1971; Deci, Koestner, & Ryan, 2001; Kohn, 1993; Ryan & Deci, 2000). Other researchers, however, have criticized both the methodology and the interpretation of results in these studies (for example, Bowen, Jenson, & Clark, 2004; Cameron & Pierce, 1994). Additionally, researchers such as Judy Cameron and W. David Pierce (1994) and K. Angeleque Akin-Little, Tanya Eckert, Benjamin Lovett, and Steven Little (2004) have conducted meta-analyses and literature reviews on this subject and found no detrimental effect of rewards on students' motivation. On the contrary, they reported that—when used appropriately—rewards and external reinforcement could facilitate learning.

The phrase "when used appropriately" is important to emphasize when using rewards. First, avoid setting too high a criterion for students to earn a reward. This is not to say that criteria for rewards should not challenge students; rather, teachers should ensure all criteria are realistic and appropriate for students' skill levels. Additionally, ensure that the criterion for success changes in response to changes in student behavior. That is, as a student or class becomes more successful and meets a goal, the teacher increases the rigor required to meet the goal the next time. Second, refrain from administering rewards to students who participate without completing the task or meeting clearly established criteria for quality of work. Criteria should be reasonable but should not be lowered after the fact if students do not meet them. Students who earn a reward for *almost* meeting a criterion may not be motivated to continue improving their performance (Akin-Little et al., 2004; Cameron & Pierce, 1994). Students will devalue the reward if it is given without meeting the predetermined criterion; in turn, there may be limited behavioral change. Finally, consistently tie tangible rewards to natural consequences and social praise. This allows for a gradual phasing out of tangible rewards as students begin to master the behavior skill (Cameron, Banko, & Pierce, 2001; Pierce & Cameron, 2006). Here, we explore three types of rewards: short-term, long-term, and intermittent rewards.

Short-Term Rewards

Short-term rewards are daily, frequent reinforcements. A short-term reward is a small, inexpensive item—such as a paper ticket, sticker, or token—that a teacher gives to an individual student immediately after that student displays behavior that meets the expectations. The short-term rewards are given to students to clearly signal to them that they are following the expectations and displaying positive behavior. However, these rewards are not simply given out to make students feel good. Instead, they serve a functional purpose in that they strengthen the learning of the expectations and provide feedback to students on their behavior. For short-term rewards to be effective, they must be paired with behavior-specific praise. Over time, the use of short-term rewards will become less frequent as students become fluent with the expectations; that is, as students master behaviors, develop intrinsic motivation to display them, and gain access to natural reinforcement, the use of short-term rewards should decrease or even become unnecessary (Akin-Little et al., 2004; Bowen et al., 2004; Partin et al., 2010).

Students save and accumulate short-term rewards in order to acquire intermittent or long-term rewards. The most important thing to remember about administering short-term rewards is that they must always occur in conjunction with behavior-specific praise; that is, when a teacher gives a short-term reward to a student, he or she must first tell that student exactly what he or she did to earn the reward. To reinforce the behavior of a student who is working quietly, for instance, a teacher might say, "I see you're being very respectful of others by working quietly at your desk. That's great! Here's a token." Focus on emphasizing a student's behavior and effort—rather than emphasizing the reward—by offering praise first.

Teachers should also keep the following tips in mind when designing and distributing short-term rewards (see also Colvin, 2007; Gable et al., 2009; George et al. 2009).

- When first teaching and reinforcing expectations, pass out short-term rewards easily and frequently. Teachers may be inclined to wait for exemplary behavior to give out short-term rewards, but should initially set easily attainable goals. Being generous at the outset builds buy-in among students (that is, they trust that the new behavior will lead to a reward) and ensures that the connection between the behavior and the reward is established. Once students demonstrate mastery, raise the criteria required to earn a reward.

- Try to expect the same standards for all students, rather than accepting only exemplary behavior from certain students and lowering standards for others. Reinforce effort for learning the expectations and reward progress accordingly.

- Take steps to avoid counterfeiting, such as using a unique type of paper for tickets, stamping the date beside signatures, changing the color of tokens each quarter, and so on.

- Do not allow students to ask for short-term rewards.

- Once a student has earned a short-term reward, refrain from taking it back as a punishment.

- Pay attention to appropriate behavior as much as possible to encourage it. Whenever a misbehaving student corrects his or her behavior, offer immediate praise and provide a short-term reward.

- If necessary, save reinforcement for occasions or lesson segments during which behavior issues most commonly arise. There is no inherent need to use it all day; it can be implemented strategically.

The goal is ultimately to gradually reduce the use of short-term rewards and, eventually, reinforce students solely with praise rather than with a combination of praise and reward. Figure 4.1 (page 54) illustrates this process.

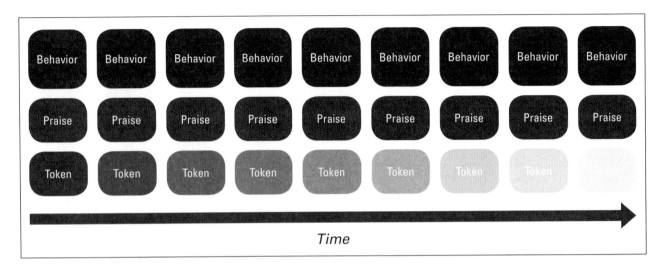

Figure 4.1: The gradual reduction of short-term rewards in the classroom.

As a real-world example of this gradual phasing out of rewards, consider a positive lifestyle habit that is difficult to maintain, such as exercising regularly. When someone who has not exercised in months wants to develop the habit of working out, her motivation will likely be low at first. As an incentive, she tells herself that if she goes to the gym, she can treat herself to a smoothie, and if she goes all week, she will earn a pedicure. At first, she creates some kind of external motivation or reinforcement—a smoothie and a pedicure—for completing the behavior. Over time, however, she notices positive natural consequences associated with exercising—her muscles become more powerful, and she feels stronger and healthier. At this point, she no longer needs external reinforcement. Her new behavior has gradually taken on intrinsic value, and she develops internal motivation to perform it. Teaching new behaviors to students in the classroom can follow a similar trajectory. At first, students may need incentives to meet expectations, but if they are implemented well, students will develop intrinsic motivation to perform them (Akin-Little et al., 2004).

There are a number of factors to consider when designing a short-term reward. For one, choose a short-term reward that is small and efficient to hand out. This portability is particularly important when students first learn a new behavior because the teacher should initially flood students with praise and short-term rewards in order to build buy-in and development of the expectation. Students are learning new skills, so they need a high rate of extrinsic reinforcement in the early stages (George et al., 2009). Teachers should also consider how often students will redeem the short-term rewards they have accrued in exchange for larger rewards and whether to publicly display students' rewards. Decide how short-term rewards will be recorded and stored. Specifically, each individual student could collect and keep track of his or her own short-term rewards, or all students' short-term rewards could be displayed publicly in the classroom.

Teachers whose students track and store their own rewards might give each student a personal manila folder, plastic file, envelope, or sandwich bag in which to keep short-term rewards. Students then store the container in their desks. These work well for paper tickets, one of the most commonly used forms of short-term rewards (George et al., 2009; Taylor-Greene et al., 1997). Tickets can be geared toward different grade levels and usually include a place for the student's name, a list of classroom expectations, and a space to indicate the routine, location, or event during which the student earned the ticket. Some teachers also circle or mark the ticket to show which expectation the student has received it for. Figure 4.2 displays several examples of tickets.

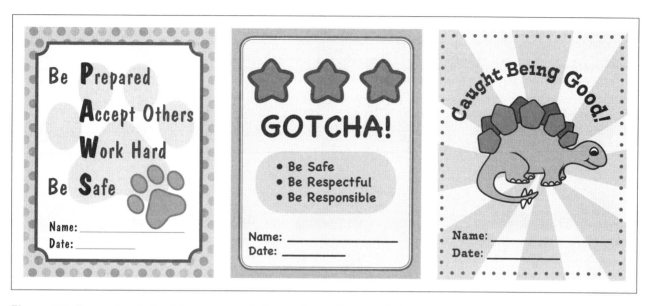

Figure 4.2: Example of short-term rewards in the form of paper tickets.

Other items that students can collect as short-term rewards include plastic chips, fake coins, and tokens. Alternatively, students can use their academic planners or handouts affixed to their desks to track teacher signatures, stamps, or stickers. As another option, teachers could log student rewards in an electronic database. Figure 4.3 shows an example of a page students might use to record short-term rewards in the form of teacher signatures.

Wrigley Middle School	Respect Self		Respect Others		Respect Our School	
	Date	Signature	Date	Signature	Date	Signature
Week One Total _____ Teacher Initials _____	_____	_____	_____	_____	_____	_____
Week Two Total _____ Teacher Initials _____	_____	_____	_____	_____	_____	_____
Week Three Total _____ Teacher Initials _____	_____	_____	_____	_____	_____	_____

Figure 4.3: Student handout for tracking short-term rewards in the form of teacher signatures.

Source: J. Ancina & J. Annand, personal communication, December 10, 2014. Used with permission.

Rather than ask students to collect physical items in a folder or marks on a handout, teachers could also display short-term rewards prominently in the classroom. Examples include adding marks next to student names on a bulletin board or adding beans to jars labeled with students' names. Figure 4.4 depicts an example of publicly displayed short-term rewards.

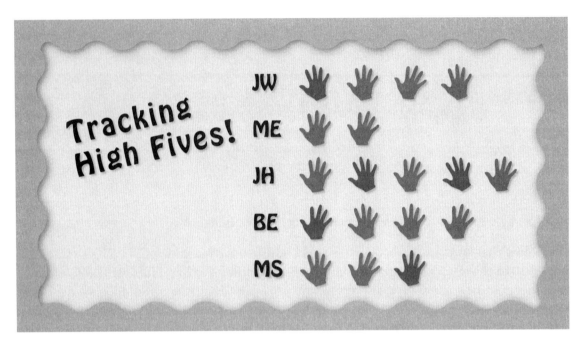

Figure 4.4: Short-term rewards in the form of public classroom displays.

Teachers can use the pros and cons listed in table 4.2 to select an effective design for their short-term rewards.

Table 4.2: Pros and Cons for Various Types of Short-Term Rewards

Type	Pros	Cons
Paper Ticket	Easy to distribute Easy to create, modify, and reproduce Can be written on	Printing costs money Not durable (easily torn or ruined)
Stamps	Easy to distribute No printing or paper cost Easily displayed	Ink costs money Could inadvertently be cleaned off
Stickers	Tangible Easily displayed	Stickers cost money
Signatures	Very inexpensive More age appropriate for older students	Difficult to minimize counterfeiting
Public Display	All students can see them Easy for teachers to track	Less optimal for students who prefer private praise

Use of short-term rewards includes ensuring that all students have access to them and receive them. Some students will require more frequent rewards than others in order to display the expectations consistently. Teachers should examine how many rewards students are receiving and make adjustments to ensure all students receive them.

Along with behavior-specific praise, short-term rewards form the foundation of the reinforcement system. These small but frequent acknowledgments of appropriate behavior keep students on the right track on a daily (and even hourly) basis and allow students to work toward larger long-term rewards.

Long-Term Rewards

Long-term rewards are prizes or celebrations that students earn over an extended period of time. Students earn these rewards by displaying positive behavior for longer periods of time or redeeming a certain number of short-term rewards. Long-term rewards can be awarded individually (that is, every student who meets the criterion earns the prize) or via group contingency (if the group as a whole meets a criterion, then the entire group earns the reward). Table 4.3 provides examples and descriptions of long-term rewards.

Table 4.3: Examples of Long-Term Rewards

Example	Description
Class Party	Students earn a celebration or party (such as a pizza party, pancake breakfast, or dance party).
Class Store	Students can purchase various items from a class store.
Raffles	Students enter raffles for certain items or activities.
Organized Activities	Students earn time to participate in an organized activity, such as a basketball game between teachers and students, kickball during recess, or a study hall before or after school.
School Tickets	Students earn tickets to school events, such as sporting events, fine arts performances, and dances.
Lunch Privileges	Students earn the privilege of eating lunch at a special table in the cafeteria or in the classroom with a teacher and a friend.

The second example in table 4.3, the class store, allows students to use the tickets, tokens, or stickers they have earned to "purchase" tangible items. Store items can include school supplies (such as pens, erasers, and notebooks), appropriate books or magazines, healthy snacks, small toys, and so on. For schools that lack a budget to spend on tangible prizes, the store might offer privilege passes. For example, a student might exchange a number of short-term rewards for a pass to be first in line at lunch or earn ten extra minutes of recess or free time. A school or teacher can adapt these privileges to suit logistical or budgetary needs. Table 4.4 (pages 58–59) displays a menu of potential prizes and privileges that could be offered in a class or school store.

Table 4.4: Sample Menu of Prizes Students Can Buy From a Class Store

Cost	Prize	Description
1 ticket	Raffle	Students can buy tickets to enter a raffle.
	Front of the line pass	Students can buy a pass that allows them to go to the front of the class line, lunch line, and so on.
5 tickets	School supplies	Students can purchase items such as pens, pencils, notebooks, highlighters, erasers, and so on.
	Hat day pass	Students can buy a pass that allows them to wear a hat all day in school.
10 tickets	Sit in the teacher's chair for an hour	Students can buy time to sit in the teacher's chair (the teacher decides whether the chair stays at the teacher's desk during this time).
	Free choice pass	Students take ten minutes of teacher-approved free choice time (to read, use the computer, and so on) during noninstructional time.
	Tardy pass	Students buy a pass that allows them to be a maximum of two minutes late to class.
	Work with a buddy pass	Students buy a pass that allows them to work with a classmate on an assignment (each student still completes his or her own assignment).
15 tickets	Music pass	Students buy a pass that allows them to use headphones for fifteen minutes during individual work time.
	Seat change pass	Students buy a pass that allows them to change seats for a class or block.
20 tickets	Helper pass	Students can purchase a pass that allows them to be a lunchroom, office, custodial, or teacher helper.
	Student-teacher lunch	Students eat lunch with a friend and the teacher.
	Gym time	Students can shoot baskets in the gym with a teacher or peers before or after school.
30 tickets	Show and tell pass	Students can buy time (three to five minutes) to show an item or tell a story in front of the class.
	Extra time	Students buy extra time at recess, in the computer lab, and so on.
	Student-administrator lunch	Students eat lunch with a friend and an administrator.
	School clothing	Students can purchase school pride clothing (T-shirts, sweatshirts, and so on) at the school store.

Cost	Prize	Description
50 tickets	Parking pass	High school students who drive cars can purchase a parking pass for the school's parking lot.
	Whole-class reward	Students buy a reward (such as extra free time or a day of no homework) for the entire class.
100 tickets	Gift certificates or coupons for local vendors	Students can buy gift certificates or coupons for nearby restaurants, shops, or entertainment facilities (such as mini golf courses or movie theaters). Local establishments are sometimes willing to offer these to teachers and schools for free or at a bulk or discounted price.

When selecting and pricing prizes, keep in mind that you may need to adjust the "cost" of items throughout the year. Because items will likely need to be replenished throughout the year, avoid placing all the high-interest items in the store during the first week of school. If all the popular items are purchased within the first few weeks of school, students may lose interest in the remaining items. Keep track of the most popular items at a school store and pay attention to the ones students talk about most.

Intermittent Rewards

Intermittent rewards are unpredictable, surprise activities or items that students earn at seemingly random times. Teachers can award an intermittent reward to students who have accumulated a certain number of short-term rewards (for example, all students who have earned ten tickets can cross out one math problem on the homework assignment) or based on students' performance during an event (for example, the students who lined up silently today can be first in line tomorrow). Students do not need to "spend" short-term rewards in order to earn an intermittent reward, even when it is contingent on the number of short-term rewards a student has accumulated. Intermittent rewards can help a teacher create a sense of suspense and rejuvenate students' awareness of the expectations. Table 4.5 (page 60) lists examples of intermittent rewards teachers can use. When used in combination with short- and long-term rewards, intermittent rewards are an effective strategy and can help maintain student buy-in to the reward system.

Group Contingencies

Group contingencies reinforce expectations by rewarding all students simultaneously. Group contingencies can overlap with other types of rewards; teachers might design group contingencies that are intermittent rewards, long-term rewards, or obtainable by exchanging short-term rewards. In some ways, group contingencies can be the most powerful reinforcers that teachers use. Scott Stage and David Quiroz (1997) conducted a meta-analysis of research on how well various interventions reduce disruptive behavior. Of all the interventions they studied, group contingencies had the largest effect size (–1.02; note that a negative effect size indicates a decrease in disruptive behavior). Teachers can use three different types of group contingencies: (1) interdependent, (2) dependent, and (3) independent.

Interdependent Group Contingencies

During an interdependent group contingency, the entire class receives a reward if the whole class reaches the goal or meets the criterion. For example, an entire class might earn a day of no homework if every student earns sixty short-term rewards in a two-week period. In such a case, every single student's performance contributes to the entire group's access to the reward.

Table 4.5: Intermittent Rewards

Reward	Description
Being First	Allow students who have earned a certain number of short-term rewards to be first during certain activities (such as being first in line for lunch, first when sharing work in front of the class, and so on).
Trophies and Symbols	Use trophies and symbols to show that a student or group has met the expectations (such as placing a golden trash can near students' desks to indicate that they had the cleanest area at the end of the day).
Ribbons and Badges	Give students each a badge or ribbon to wear for a day to show that they have met the expectations for three consecutive days.
In-Class Privileges	Allow students who earned a certain amount of short-term rewards to have special privileges (such as sitting in the teacher's chair, wearing hats, or chewing gum) during class.
Independent Work Time Privileges	Allow students who earned a certain number of short-term rewards to have special privileges (such as listening to music or sitting with friends) during independent work time.
Public Recognition	Prompt all students to clap and cheer for a classmate once he or she reaches a certain goal.

A popular interdependent group contingency is the mystery motivator; the class does not know what their reward will be until they earn it. The mystery motivator can be small, such as a few minutes of all-class free time, or much larger, such as playing a whole-class game or participating in an ice cream party. Erinn Musser, Melissa Bray, Thomas Kehle, and William Jenson (2001) described a variation of the mystery motivator. The teacher identifies a specific behavior to target (for example, demonstrating active listening during a lesson) and then tells students they can earn points for displaying the target behavior. Once students earn a certain number of points, they earn the mystery reward. To enhance suspense and provide a visual reminder for students, the teacher writes the reward on a card, seals it in an envelope labeled with a question mark, and then publicly displays the envelope at the front of the room. The teacher then designates a certain time period in which students have the chance to earn points. For instance, students might only be able to earn points during a math block or during independent seat work. During that designated time, the teacher provides behavior-specific praise and awards points to students, tracking the points earned on a poster, chalkboard, or whiteboard. Once the class has accumulated the target number of points, the class earns the reward.

Dependent Group Contingencies

For a dependent group contingency, a teacher rewards the whole class for the success of one student or small group of students. For example, a teacher awards an entire class a day of no homework if two designated students earn ten short-term rewards within a two-week period. Dependent group contingencies can help build momentum and provide support for individual students who struggle with behavior; still, teachers must take steps to ensure that the class does not become upset with the target students if they do not earn the reward. Teachers can avoid this by discussing with the class how to respond when the reward is not earned and practicing how to respond appropriately.

One example of a dependent group contingency is the chance jar (Theodore, Bray, Kehle, & Jenson, 2001). As with the mystery motivator described previously, the teacher identifies a time period, a behavior to target, and a criterion (for example, five tickets). The teacher explains that each time students display the expectation, they can earn a ticket. At the end of the designated time period, the teacher draws one slip of paper out of each of two jars. One jar contains individual slips of paper labeled with different whole-class rewards. The second jar contains individual slips of paper labeled with each student's name. If the student whose name is drawn has met the criterion, then the whole class earns the reward.

Independent Group Contingencies

Finally, in an independent group contingency, each student earns the group reward based on his or her individual behavior. Essentially, this is a reward that is standard for all students. Every student has the same chance at earning the same reward. For example, a teacher may offer a no homework pass to any student who earns ten tokens within a week. In this way, independent group contingencies are very similar to long-term rewards.

As an example of how a teacher might use independent group contingencies, the teacher might start by defining a target behavior for students to perform. Throughout the day or lesson, students receive teacher feedback on their behavior. When praised, a student draws one smiley face on his or her tracking sheet. When a student displays unwanted behavior, the teacher offers a warning and a chance for the student to correct the behavior. If the student continues the negative behavior, he or she draws a sad face on the tracking sheet. At the end of the instructional period, the students with more smiley faces than sad faces earn the reward.

Designing an Effective Reinforcement System

To design a reinforcement system, teachers can start by identifying those things that students find motivating and reinforcing. This process might involve simple interviews, whole-class discussions, or short surveys with students. Ask them to brainstorm prizes or class activities they might like to earn for meeting classroom expectations, but be sure to indicate that not all of their ideas will actually turn into possible rewards. Teachers can preface the session by saying that students should be reasonable with their requests and that they are not guaranteed to get what they requested. Allow them to bring up ideas for reinforcers and list them. This can be done publicly in a class discussion or privately by having students write down what they want to earn. After the students generate a list, the teacher organizes the usable ideas into four categories: (1) short-term rewards, (2) long-term rewards, (3) intermittent rewards, and (4) group contingencies. Table 4.6 (page 62) depicts an organized list of reward ideas from a student brainstorming session.

In addition to soliciting ideas for rewards from students and using the ideas presented in this book, teachers can consult various resources for more ideas on short-term, long-term, intermittent, and group contingency rewards. A number of books, websites, and organizations (such as the following) offer ideas for classroom rewards.

- *Applied Behavior Analysis for Teachers* (9th ed.) (Alberto & Troutman, 2013)

- *School-Based Interventions for Students With Behavior Problems* (Bowen et al., 2004)

- *Effective School Interventions* (Rathvon, 1999)

- Intervention Central (www.interventioncentral.org)

- Technical Assistance Center on Positive Behavioral Interventions and Supports (www.pbis.org)

- PBIS World (www.pbisworld.com)

Table 4.6: Organized List of Reward Examples

Type of Reward	Examples
Short Term	Paper tickets (paired with behavior-specific praise) students use to purchase rewards from the school store Teacher signatures (paired with behavior-specific praise) students use to purchase rewards from the school store
Long Term	Large-item raffle (for example, lunch delivered to student, tickets to an event, donated items from local stores, and so on) Whole-class celebration (movie party, pizza party, bring a board game to school to play)
Intermittent	All students who earned a ticket during the day are first to line up at the door All students who earned a ticket during a class period allowed to leave two minutes early for lunch Students who earned a set number of tickets allowed first choice for an activity or task
Group Contingencies	Weekly rewards based on total tokens earned by the whole class for a specific expectation Two designated students who earn five tokens for being responsible during a class period earn the class ten minutes of free time during next day's class

Teachers can use a matrix such as the one in table 4.7 to define the types of rewards they would like to use in their classrooms and how they will be used. A blank version of this matrix is available in "Matrix for Designing Rewards in a Reinforcement System" (page 68).

Table 4.7: Completed Matrix for Designing Rewards in a Reinforcement System

Type of Reward	Type Used in Class	Description	Distribution Details
Short Term	Paper tickets	I will give behavior-specific praise and hand out tickets that list expectations to students.	Every day
Long Term	Class store	I will call students to the store in groups of three and allow them to redeem their tickets.	Store time every Monday during afternoon recess
Intermittent	Early lineup	I will allow all students who earned tickets during a specified time to line up at the door first.	Occasionally (once or twice per week)
Group Contingencies	Mystery motivator	If the class collects enough tickets, I will give all students one of four rewards (a day of no home-work, an extra ten minutes of recess, a pajama day, or a pass to listen to music).	Once every few weeks

Source: Adapted from Florida's Positive Behavior Support Project, n.d.

One challenge of designing and implementing an effective reinforcement system is remembering to consistently recognize students for meeting expectations. Accordingly, many teachers benefit from systems that remind them to distribute short-term rewards. Research supports the use of teacher self-monitoring strategies, such as graphing the number of tokens a teacher passes out on a given day

(Reinke et al., 2013; Reinke et al., 2007; Reinke, Lewis-Palmer, & Merrell, 2008; Simonsen, Myers, & DeLuca, 2010). Teachers can choose to focus on monitoring reinforcement of a particular expectation, procedure, or student. For example, a teacher may decide on a Monday that, during that week, he or she will focus on praising all students for showing respect. Teachers can apply this same concept to particular students who struggle to receive praise or to a certain routine in which students need more feedback to become successful. Here, we describe a few strategies that help teachers monitor their use of reinforcement and rewards.

Structured Games

Create a structured game that emphasizes particular expectations, and use it to monitor the distribution of student rewards. One example of a structured game is the mystery motivator game (page 60). The following six steps can provide structure for teachers who want to create their own versions of these games.

1. Identify an expectation that students need to work on, a time period in which they need the most improvement, and a criterion for a reward. For example, a teacher might decide that students need to work on raising their hands instead of calling out during teacher-led instruction, and set the criterion that students must have more than ten instances of the correct behavior to earn a reward.

2. Divide the class into teams. For example, the classroom could be divided down the center to create two teams, or, if students sit in clusters at desks or tables, each table can be a team. Students can play individually, but it is likely more effective and efficient when students are in teams because the teams create social norms and expectations (Anhalt et al., 1998; Bowen et al., 2004; Theodore et al., 2001).

3. Teach students the expectation (see page 44).

4. Create a simple, visual system for each team (or individual student) to use to record the praise they earn for meeting expectations, such as tally marks or stickers on a team poster or section of the chalkboard. Each tally mark or other symbol equates to one instance of correct behavior and praise, and one "point" within the game.

5. Throughout the time period, recognize the desired behavior and provide behavior-specific praise (see page 50) to students for meeting expectations. Mark each instance of behavior on the student or team's visual tracker using a tally mark (elementary teachers might use a small symbol, such as a smiley face, star, and so on). In the example from step 1, for instance, the teacher would give praise and mark a tally on the appropriate team's chart each time a student raised his or her hand to contribute instead of calling out.

6. At the end of the time period, provide a group reward based on the predetermined criterion for tallies earned.

These steps are typically used over a short period of time within one day. For example, an elementary school teacher may use a structured game during reading block, or a secondary teacher could use a game during the teacher-led portion of class. Creating a structured game has several benefits. First, these steps include instruction and reinforcement and therefore serve as a way to teach students skills and behaviors (see Anhalt et al., 1998). Second, the steps can help teachers practice frequently praising students. That is, a structured game focuses the teacher's attention on giving praise and acknowledging students for positive behavior. The visual point-tracking system also serves as a visual cue to praise. Finally, this game generates easy-to-use data for teachers. Teachers can examine the number of tally marks or praise statements earned to make inferences about trends in student behavior, observations about their own progress with regard to teaching and reinforcing behavior, and decisions about how to proceed. Finally, the game structure is adaptable and flexible. It can be used with a wide range of behaviors in any class. Teachers can play this game briefly during the day (for example, for thirty minutes), or it can be adapted for use across longer periods of time.

Cues

Teachers can use visual or physical reminders—called *cues*—to remind themselves to praise students. For example, teachers can identify a certain number of praise statements they want to give out, such as ten statements during a lesson. The teacher can then carry ten small objects—such as coins—in one pocket. On reaching into the pocket and noticing the coins, the teacher gives a praise statement, and then moves a coin to a different pocket. After all ten coins have been moved from one pocket to the other, the teacher knows he or she has reached the goal. To vary this method, place several pieces of brightly colored tape (or adhesive flags, paperclips, and so on) on the corner of a lecture stand or projector during direct instruction. Move the tape from one side of the stand to the other after giving a praise statement to keep track of how many have been given. Alternatively, the teacher can simply place a note within view as a reminder to praise. Whenever the teacher looks at the note, she can remind herself to praise correct behavior. Finally, set timers or program beepers to prompt the use of praise. Use technology tools such as a smartphone alarm, a reminder app, or a small pager to provide regular cues.

Another option is to place a visual cue card on each student's desk. This method not only provides a visual cue for a teacher to give praise, but also generates data to use in tracking the effectiveness of the program as a whole. Label index cards or small pieces of paper with a number of blank checkboxes, a short description of the expectation, an explicit skill related to the expectation, and at least two behaviors that students can perform to properly demonstrate that skill. Figure 4.5 depicts an example of such a card.

The cue card in figure 4.5 focuses on the expectation "Be respectful" and, specifically, the skill of active listening. It lists four concrete behaviors students can perform in order to listen actively. During class, the teacher praises students who demonstrate active listening and these students mark one of the boxes on their individual cue cards. For example, a teacher might say, "I see Mary using active listening by looking at me while I'm talking. Mary, mark off one of the boxes on your card." When the student has checked off all five boxes, she places the card on the teacher's desk and takes a new, blank one. After instruction, the teacher signs all the completed cards and places them in a basket. Each student receives one short-term reward for each cue card he or she completes. Additionally, teachers can use cue cards to create a group contingency. When the class as a whole earns a certain number of cards, the teacher awards a prize to the whole class. Use completed cards as data to determine which students need further attention or support in meeting expectations.

Student: Mary K.

Expectation: Be respectful

Key Skill: Active listening

☐ ☐ ☐ ☐ ☐

Behaviors:

- Eyes on the speaker

- Four chair legs on the floor

- Voice off

- Raise hand to speak

Figure 4.5: A visual cue card for monitoring and tracking reinforcement.

Source: W. Malmed, personal communication, April 17, 2014. Used with permission.

Colleague Observations

Ask a colleague to observe the rate of reinforcement in your classroom. When a colleague observes, he or she stays in the classroom for ten to twenty minutes and marks a tally for each praise statement or short-term reward given in that time period. The colleague also records any redirections or negative statements given during the observation. Such observations provide teachers with information about how frequently they use reinforcement strategies, as well as a ratio of positive to negative statements. If no colleague can take time to observe, teachers can video- or audio-record part of a lesson and analyze the recording after class. Teachers can also display the total tallies in a bar graph to make the data easier to analyze. "Colleague Observation Guide for Monitoring and Tracking Student Praise" (page 69) provides an observation template.

Student Peer Monitoring

Teachers can also share responsibility for monitoring praise and rewards with students through the use of class objects, pay-it-forward rewards, and prompts to look out for certain behaviors. In the first strategy, the teacher places a class object—such as a trophy, stuffed animal, or bobblehead—on a student's desk to show that he or she has met expectations. Within twenty-four hours, that student must pass the object to another student who has met expectations. The class object method serves the threefold purpose of providing an ongoing visual reminder of the expectations, recognizing students for their behavior, and creating a peer-to-peer recognition system. Teaching students how and when to pass along the object is important for this activity to operate smoothly. For example, a teacher might instruct students to pass the object during transition times and explain to the recipient why he or she is receiving it. A second way to encourage students to peer monitor involves teaching them a pay-it-forward aspect to receiving short-term rewards; that is, when one student receives a reward, he or she pays it forward by giving a reward to someone else. For example, a teacher who gives paper tickets as short-term rewards might reserve space on each ticket for students to cut off and give away, as shown on the ticket in figure 4.6 (page 66). The pay-it-forward method eases the demand on the teacher to pass out rewards. It also facilitates a social norm in which students praise each other for positive behavior. Finally, a teacher can instruct students to look out for a certain behavior. When students see this behavior, they praise the student who performed it. They might also give out differently colored peer tokens or tickets to signify their praise.

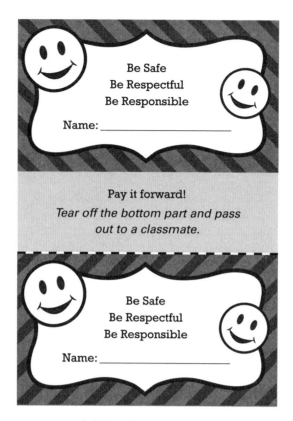

Figure 4.6: Example of a short-term reward ticket that includes a pay-it-forward option.

Summary

This chapter discussed different types of reinforcement and examples of ways to reinforce students' behavior. The reinforcement of expectations is an important part of classroom management because it provides the instructional feedback students need to learn and display the expectations. There are three types of reinforcement teachers can use: (1) behavior-specific praise, (2) rewards, and (3) group contingencies. As part of a comprehensive system of reinforcement, teachers might set up cues or reminders to help them give out a certain number of praise statements or short-term rewards, such as creating a structured game, using a cue, or having a colleague observe and give feedback. Students can also partake in reinforcement by noticing and recognizing peers' behavior. In addition to reinforcement, teachers can also use active engagement to manage behavior in the classroom. The next chapter discusses ways to increase student engagement.

Chapter 4: Comprehension Questions

1. What are examples of each type of reinforcement?

2. What are the critical elements of behavior-specific praise?

3. What are some things to consider when designing rewards?

4. Describe the three types of group contingency.

Matrix for Designing Rewards in a Reinforcement System

Type of Reward	Type Used in Class	Description	Distribution Details
Short Term			
Long Term			
Intermittent			
Group Contingencies			

Source: Adapted from Florida's Positive Behavior Support Project. (n.d.). Accessed at http://flpbs.fmhi.usf.edu/index.cfm on December 2, 2014.

Colleague Observation Guide for Monitoring and Tracking Student Praise

Date of observation: _____

Start time: _____

End time: _____

Total minutes: _____

Classroom activity: _____

Place a tally mark for every praise statement (general and behavior specific) and redirect for student behavior (you may wish to include academic statements as well).

	General Praise (for example, "Nice work!")	Behavior-Specific Praise (for example, "Johnny, you are sitting quietly. Well done.")	Redirects (for example, "Johnny, please sit up straight, and put your eyes on me.")
Tally Marks			
Totals			

Total praise: _____ [general praise] + _____ [behavior-specific praise] = _____ [total praise]

Proximity to the magic ratio: _____ [total praise] ÷ _____ [total redirects] = _____ to 1

Chapter 5

ACTIVELY ENGAGING STUDENTS

An important element of an effective classroom management system is students' engagement with academic content. When students actively respond to tasks or content, they have less time to engage in problem behavior (Partin et al., 2010; Sutherland & Wehby, 2001), and academic success helps foster socially appropriate classroom behavior (Lewis et al., 2004; Sutherland & Wehby, 2001). *Active student engagement* refers to instruction during which students are required to produce a response, such as answering questions verbally or writing responses. *Passive student engagement* is the opposite; students listen to the instruction and take a passive role in the learning. This chapter reviews how to effectively prompt students to respond, as well as practical strategies teachers can use to increase the response rates in their classrooms.

Opportunities to Respond

When a student responds to an academic question or task, the teacher gains information about the student's mastery of content. The teacher also has a chance to correct any errors in the student's thinking and to provide another opportunity to perform the skill correctly. Consequently, teachers can increase the level of active engagement in their classrooms by giving students many *opportunities to respond* (OTRs)—chances to answer or complete an academically oriented question or task (Brophy & Good, 1986). In fact, the level of active engagement within a classroom can be quantified by measuring the number of OTRs students have.

When used properly, OTRs can help keep students engaged, reduce rates of misbehavior, and improve academic outcomes (Brophy & Good, 1986; Partin et al., 2010; Sutherland & Wehby, 2001). The effective use of OTRs includes efficient error correction and a high rate of OTRs.

Correcting Errors

One element of using OTRs effectively involves maintaining a lively pace while also correcting student misunderstandings. When teachers use OTRs, they trigger *learning trials*. These are brief interactions between students and teachers that consist of three steps: (1) a teacher prompt, (2) a student response, and (3) teacher feedback (Brophy & Good, 1986; Partin et al., 2010; Simonsen et al., 2010). Figure 5.1 (page 72) depicts the three components of a learning trial.

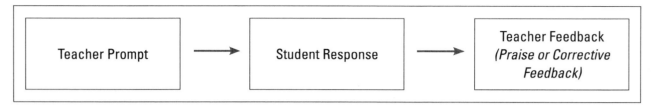

Figure 5.1: Three components of a learning trial.

Source: Adapted from Haydon, Marsicano, & Scott, 2013.

The following verbal exchange between a teacher and students exemplifies a simple learning trial.

Teacher: [pointing to the whiteboard] Class, what word is this?

Class: Hope!

Teacher: That's right. The word is *hope.*

In this example, the teacher prompts the entire class to respond and then provides feedback (in this case, praise). Between a prompt and a student response, the teacher also provides wait time (a brief amount of time given to students to process information). Ashley S. MacSuga-Gage, Brandi Simonsen, and Don Briere (2012) recommended that teachers give students between three and five seconds of wait time before prompting them to respond. Teachers should also be sure to match learning trials to students' instructional levels (neither too easy nor too difficult) to encourage engagement and avoid too many incorrect answers (Brophy & Good, 1986; Treptow, Burns, & McComas, 2007).

If students do respond incorrectly during a learning trial, the teacher provides an error correction (Watkins & Slocum, 2004). In an error correction, the teacher immediately gives the correct answer to the student, offers a second OTR, and then proceeds with instruction.

Teacher: [pointing to the whiteboard] Class, what word is this?

Class: [indiscernible mumbling]

Teacher: The word is *hope.* What's the word?

Class: Hope!

Teacher: That's right. The word is *hope.*

Here, the teacher prompts the class ("What word is this?"), waits for a response (indiscernible mumbling), provides an error correction ("The word is *hope.*"), and then prompts the class again ("What's the word?"), waits for a response, and provides praise. Although this example shows a teacher providing an error correction on academic content, teachers can also use this strategy with behavior. For example, a teacher may ask a group of students who run down the hallway to walk back, turn around, and walk down the hallway properly.

Efficient error correction ensures that the teacher maintains the pace of instruction when a student gives an incorrect answer, thereby maintaining a high rate of OTRs. The teacher gives corrective feedback and gives the student a chance to practice the correct answer, and instruction continues without losing momentum. Although discussing a mistake or prompting students to use certain strategies to arrive at the correct answer can be helpful at times, students can lose interest or become confused when extended time is given to errors. Instead, time is better spent practicing the correct skill. Generally speaking, spending a few seconds on error correction is more beneficial than spending a minute or two discussing the wrong answer or waiting for students to arrive at the correct answer (Heward, 1997).

Frequent Opportunities to Respond

As previously stated, high rates of OTRs benefit students' learning and are associated with increases in task engagement and decreases in behavioral disruptions (Carnine, 1976; Haydon et al., 2010; Sutherland, Alder, & Gunter, 2003; Sutherland & Wehby, 2001). Providing an adequate rate of OTRs during a lesson engages students, affords opportunities to check their understanding of content, and facilitates the frequent use of behavior-specific praise. Therefore, teachers should establish and maintain an effective rate of OTRs in the classroom.

Researchers recommend that when teachers introduce new content, they provide, on average, four to six OTRs every minute, with students answering correctly at least 80 percent of the time. When reviewing previously learned material, teachers should use a rate of eight to twelve OTRs per minute, with students answering correctly at least 90 percent of the time (Council for Exceptional Children, 1987; Gunter, Reffel, Barnett, Lee, & Patrick, 2004; Johnson & Layng, 1994; Sutherland & Wehby, 2001). OTR rates also vary depending on the instructional format a teacher is using. For whole-class instruction, researchers recommend between three and six OTRs per minute versus eight to twelve for small-group instruction (Carnine, 1976; Gunter et al., 2004; Harlacher, Walker, & Sanford, 2010). Students with disabilities may require at least ten OTRs per minute in order to learn the content (Gunter et al., 2004; Haydon et al., 2009).

These rates of OTRs may seem high, but—given the fact that OTRs vary significantly in length—they are feasible. For example, one long student response can actually count as several responses. Consider a teacher who prompts students to write and share an answer. This practice provides several OTRs in one instance. The student is given a prompt to think about what to write (one OTR), then instructed to write down his or her thought (second OTR), and then told to share what he or she wrote with a classmate (third OTR). As a second example, having a student read a paragraph aloud can be constructed as several OTRs because the student is reading several sentences (that is, each sentence might count as one OTR). Furthermore, even if a teacher does not immediately achieve optimal rates of OTRs, any increase of OTRs in the classroom can be beneficial. Kevin Sutherland, Nora Adler, and Philip Gunter (2003) found that an increase from 1.68 OTRs per minute to 3.52 OTRs per minute was associated with students giving twice as many correct responses in class, decreased disruptions, and increased task engagement.

Types of Student Responses

Although the proposed rates of OTRs (between four and six per minute for new material and eight and twelve per minute for previously learned material) may seem challenging or even impossible to implement during a lesson, teachers can employ a number of strategies to incorporate OTRs frequently and seamlessly in the classroom. OTR strategies can be broadly organized into three categories: (1) verbal responses, (2) written responses, and (3) action responses.

Verbal Responses

Verbal responses are those in which students provide a spoken response to a teacher's question or task. Types of verbal responses include individual, choral, and peer-to-peer responses. These types are briefly described in table 5.1 (page 74).

Table 5.1: Examples of OTRs and Active Engagement

Response Type	Description
Individual	The teacher calls on one student to verbally respond (for example, "Jon, what is this word?").
Choral	Students respond in unison with each other (for example, "Everyone, what is this word?").
Peer to Peer	Students work in pairs or small groups to share information verbally.

Individual Responses

To solicit an individual response, the teacher directly asks a question and calls on a student to respond independently, typically in front of the class. For example, a teacher may say, "Class, think about the product of five and two," provide some wait time, and then ask, "Laura, what is five times two?" By asking individual students to respond, students' engagement in class increases and their off-task behavior decreases because they are more actively involved. Additionally, a student's response provides a teacher with feedback on the student's mastery of content; if the student answers correctly, the teacher knows the student has learned the material. If the student does not answer correctly, the teacher knows the student needs more instruction and practice (Brophy & Good, 1986; Carnine, 1976; Haydon et al., 2010; Sutherland et al., 2003; Sutherland & Wehby, 2001).

When using individual responses, teachers might sometimes want to ensure that a student provides the correct answer to a question when he or she is called on in order to prevent students from accidentally retaining incorrect information. To do this, teachers can have students write down answers or discuss them in groups before asking an individual to respond in front of the class. While students are writing and discussing, the teacher listens for correct answers—while correcting students who answer incorrectly—and then calls on a student who knows the correct response. This strategy can help teachers ensure that students acquire the correct skills and avoid receiving several consecutive wrong answers in front of the class.

Finally, teachers should minimize their use of volunteer responding, which tends to allow a handful of students to repeatedly respond and dominate the conversation. Avoid initiating an individual response with a statement such as "Who can tell me . . ." or "Does anyone know . . ." which invites volunteers to respond. Instead, teachers can call on any student at any time, even if the student did not raise his or her hand. This type of selection—called a *cold call*—helps the teacher ensure the participation of every student and keeps all students on their toes. Deliberately select particular students to answer particular questions, or randomly select students by drawing names from a cup. To prevent students from tuning out, return their names to the cup after they are drawn to incentivize students to remain attentive.

Choral Responses

Teachers can also request choral responses, in which a group of students or an entire class replies in unison. The teacher poses a question, allows sufficient wait time, and then cues the class to respond. Choral responses involve all students in instruction and provide relative security for those who do not know if their answer is correct. Compared to an individual response, therefore, a choral response can lead to higher rates of active student engagement, on-task behavior, and correct responses (Haydon et al., 2013). This is not to say that individual responding does not have its place. In fact, Todd Haydon and his colleagues (2010) recommended that, during a lesson, students respond chorally in 70 percent of cases and individually in 30 percent of cases.

Teachers can use a few different strategies to enhance the effectiveness of choral responses. First, model the procedure for choral responding to students before asking them to do it. This will help avoid chaotic and incoherent responses. Some teachers use a signal to cue choral responses, such as raising a hand after asking the question, providing a second or two of wait time, and then dropping the hand to prompt students to respond. Signals can help students respond together as a group, allow teachers to give wait time during choral responses, and keep the pace moving. Second, choral responses should have only one correct answer and be presented at a brisk pace (Heward, 1994). For example, the question, What is six times four? has one definitive answer, and so all students can call out, "Twenty-four!" in unison. Additionally, limit choral responses to a few words: "In our story, Matilda is the main character—true or false?"

One type of choral response simply involves asking students to repeat back segments of what the teacher says. Consider, for example, this excerpt from a science lesson on information processing.

Teacher: Today we're going to learn about information processing theory. What theory are we going to learn about?

Class: Information processing theory.

Teacher: Good. Information processing theory states that our memory consists of three memory storage systems. They are sensory memory, working memory, and long-term memory. Sensory, working, and long-term. What are the three storage systems?

Class: Sensory, working, and long-term.

Teacher: Right. Sensory memory is how we remember information through our senses. Working memory is the active part of memory—it's where we do all of our thinking. Long-term memory is the place we keep all of our memories and knowledge. So where do we store all of our memories?

Class: Long-term memory.

Teacher: What is the active part of our memory?

Class: Working memory.

Teacher: And what memory deals with our senses?

Class: Sensory memory.

In this example, the teacher provides five different OTRs in a relatively short period of time by asking students to repeat back the information presented to them. This allows students to actively participate throughout the lesson, rather than passively absorb information from a lecture.

Peer-to-Peer Responses

The final type of verbal response is peer-to-peer response, in which students react to a task or question in pairs or small groups. Peer-to-peer responses give students a chance to learn new ideas, receive feedback, practice cooperation skills, and communicate with others. Use peer-to-peer responses for open-ended questions or tasks to allow students to share different responses. For example, a peer-to-peer response works well with a question such as, What themes did the author use in this story? Using peer-to-peer responses with questions that only have one correct answer—such as, Which part of the cell contains genetic material?—does not allow for both students to share and discuss opinions and reasoning. This question might be more conducive to choral or individual response.

As with choral response, teach students a procedure for peer-to-peer responses. Anita Archer and Charles Hughes (2010) offered the following three steps for teaching peer-to-peer response: (1) model active listening skills, (2) provide each student in the pair with a number (one or two) or nickname (such as peanut butter or jelly), and (3) give instructions for responding (for example, "Ones, you share your answer first, and then twos, you share"). As with all procedures, practice peer-to-peer responding and offer corrective feedback to students before implementing it in a lesson.

A commonly used version of peer-to-peer response is think-pair-share (Kagan & Kagan, 2009). In think-pair-share, students individually think about a question or task, write down their thoughts, and then discuss them with a peer. Teachers can then call on pairs to share with the whole class. Alternatively, pairs can combine with other pairs to discuss their answers in groups of four, groups of four combine to form groups of eight, and so on until the paired responses transform into a whole-class discussion. Variations on think-pair-share include the look-lean-whisper (pairs make eye contact, lean toward each other, and whisper their responses) and the check-your-partner (pairs exchange written responses to see if they agreed on the answer; Archer & Hughes, 2010).

Another peer-to-peer strategy is classwide peer tutoring, which involves students reviewing information by tutoring each other in pairs (Greenwood, 1997; Greenwood, Maheady, & Delquadri, 2002). This strategy has been shown to increase engagement and achievement in reading and mathematics (Greenwood et al., 2002; Institute of Education Sciences [IES], 2007; Kamps, Barbetta, Leonard, Delquadri, & Hall, 1994; Rohrbeck, Ginsberg-Block, Fantuzzo, & Miller, 2003). First, divide students into pairs based on skill level. Do not pair the highest-performing students with the lowest-performing students; this can lead to frustration and a lack of challenge among the high performers. Instead, pair the highest-performing students with students who perform at an average level and work down from there. With this method, the highest-performing student works with the middle-of-the-pack student, the second-highest-performing student works with the student just below the middle, and so forth. Following this pattern, the lowest-performing student works with a peer who is just above the middle of the pack. For example, if there are twenty students in a class, the first-ranked student would work with the eleventh-ranked student, the second-ranked student with the twelfth-ranked student, the third with the thirteenth, and so on.

Once students have been paired, designate one student as the tutor and the other the tutee. Give them ten minutes to practice with the content. The tutor presents content to the tutee (such as a stack of math flashcards or a paragraph for the tutee to read aloud). As the tutee responds, the tutor provides praise ("Yes, that's correct!") and corrective feedback ("No, the correct answer is . . .") until time is up. When the tutee answers incorrectly, the tutor also prompts him or her to repeat the problem and answer three times. Then the students switch roles and repeat the process. Teachers can also make classwide peer tutoring into a game. Students earn two tally marks for each correct answer and one tally mark for correcting themselves after an incorrect answer. During the game, the teacher walks around the room and provides additional points to students for staying on task, following procedures, and meeting classroom expectations. When the session ends, each pair reports the total number of points they earned and the teacher records each team's points on a poster at the front of the room. The pair with the most points wins.

Written Responses

Written responses involve students writing a response on paper or another medium (for example, a whiteboard) and showing it to the teacher. Types of written responses include whiteboards, guided notes, exit slips, and text-related questions.

Whiteboards

To combine elements of choral responses with the written format, students can use individual whiteboards to write down and display their answers to a question. The teacher asks a question that has a brief response and gives students a few moments to write the answer before holding up their boards simultaneously. Students can then erase their answers and prepare for the next OTR. While whiteboards can be used with multiple-choice questions and other tasks with very short responses, they are also useful for questions with slightly longer answers or problems that require more thought. For example, students might be asked to answer a simple math problem and show their work on whiteboards.

Guided Notes

Teachers can provide students with guided notes (printed copies of notes with pieces of information missing) to help them record important information, concepts, and facts during a lesson (Heward, 1994, 1997). As the lesson progresses, students fill in the blanks on the handout with the missing pieces of information. Figure 5.2 displays an example of guided notes.

Types of Verbs
What is a verb?
A verb is used to express an: _____.
The three types of verbs are: _____, _____, and _____.
Action verbs are: _____.

Figure 5.2: Example of guided notes.

Exit Slips

Exit slips are prompts that students complete at the end of class to reflect on the lesson. Teachers commonly use exit slips as a means of assessment; however, they also have other uses. Douglas Fisher and Nancy Frey (2004) proposed three types of exit slips: (1) those that document students' learning for assessment, (2) those that emphasize the process of learning, and (3) those that allow students to evaluate the effectiveness of the instruction. Table 5.2 (page 78) provides examples of prompts teachers can use on each type of exit slip. Teachers can also use exit slips to increase engagement. Give a copy of the exit slip to students at the beginning of a lesson to prime their knowledge. Students can also share their exit slip responses with a peer, which provides another opportunity for response and reflection.

Text-Related Questions

A final way to solicit a written response from students involves prompting them to write answers to text-related questions using class texts. Provide students with a list of questions related to the reading. Ask them to read the questions before they start reading the text. Next, students preview the text and read it, answering questions as they read. Table 5.3 (page 78) outlines four different types of text-related questions teachers can ask students.

Table 5.2: Sample Prompts for Exit Slips

Type of Prompt	Example
Documenting Learning	Write one thing you learned today.
	Rate your understanding of today's knowledge from 1 to 10. How can you improve your level of knowledge?
	Discuss one way in which today's lesson can be used in the real world.
Emphasizing the Process of Learning	I didn't understand _____.
	Write one question you have about today's lesson.
	Of the two strategies you learned about, which one did you find most useful? Why?
Evaluating Effectiveness of Instruction	How did you like working in small groups today?
	The best part of class today was _____.
	I would like to learn more about _____.

Source: Adapted from Reading Rockets, n.d.

Table 5.3: Categories of Text-Related Questions for Written Responses

Category	Description	Example
Right There	Questions for which students can find the answer expressed directly in the text (often the words are the same within the text as in the question and do not require prior knowledge of the text)	Where does this person live? When does this story take place?
Think and Search	Questions that require students to gather several sources of information from different places in the text and put them together to form an answer	What are the important ideas in this text? What clues in the text help us define the word _____? How do you know this person is _____ [brave, sad, strong, and so on]?
Author and You	Questions that require students to relate information in the text to their own personal experiences	If you could interview the author about this story, what would you ask? What questions do you still have about this topic? Why do you think the author _____?
On My Own	Questions that only require the student's background knowledge—and no information from the text—to answer	Have you ever been in the situation the main character was? When was a time you felt _____ [brave, sad, strong, and so on]? What do you think about _____ [topic of the reading]?

Sources: Adapted from Fisher & Frey, 2004; Raphael & Au, 2005.

Alternatively, students can create and answer their own questions about the text. Provide sentence stems such as the following.

- What do you think would happen if _____?

- How would you compare and contrast _____?

- How do you think _____ could have been prevented?

- How would you interpret _____?

Action Responses

Students share action responses through the silent use of gestures or objects. Action responses may involve gestures, response cards, or technology tools.

Gestures

Gestures allow students to express their thoughts using body language. For example, students might use the following gestures.

- Give a thumbs-up if they understand the content, a thumbs-down if they do not, and a thumbs-sideways if they partially understand it.

- Hold up one, two, three, or four fingers to indicate their response to a multiple-choice question (one finger indicates the first choice, two fingers indicates the second choice, and so on) or to indicate their level of understanding (one finger means no understanding and four fingers means total understanding).

- Clap to indicate that they understand directions (for example, the teacher says, "When you finish your math problems, start your vocabulary work. Understand?" and the class claps once in unison).

- Pair physical gestures with lesson concepts, such as a set of gestures that symbolize the order of mathematical operations (for example, miming a slash across the body represents division, crossing arms in an X represents multiplication, and so on).

- Use facial expressions or act out certain parts of a story, vocabulary terms, or concepts (Oregon RTI, 2013).

- Point to or touch certain stimuli, in response to prompts such as "Touch the word _____ in your book" or "Point to the addition sign."

Response Cards

Response cards include slips of paper, signs, or other items students hold up in the air to share responses during instruction. For example, a teacher might give students cards labeled with the different parts of speech, ask questions about parts of speech, and prompt students to hold up different cards to signal their answers. Teachers can premake and distribute response cards (such as cards that say "True," "False," "A," "B," "C," and "D"). All students hold up their response cards at the same time for choral responses or individually for individual responses, and the teacher provides feedback. Teachers can also prompt students to share responses with each other (for example, "Show your answer to your partner"). Response cards are also a good way to combine action responses with written responses. For example, the teacher says, "Class, show me the suffix of this word using your response cards. Now write a word ending in *-ing* and show it to your partner."

Technology Tools

Finally, students can use technology tools to give action responses. Clickers, for example, allow students to press a number or letter button on the keypad and digitally transmit their choice to the teacher's computer. The clicker software program automatically tallies students' responses and displays them onscreen to students (available sets of clickers and software include MimioVote™, Got It!™, and eInstruction® models). If a teacher does not have clickers, students can access websites or apps using smartphones or tablets—such as Poll Everywhere (www.polleverywhere.com) or i>clicker (www1.iclicker.com)—to submit digital responses to questions. Whereas written responses require actively writing an answer, these tools require simply clicking, selecting, or texting a response.

Tracking Opportunities to Respond

Teachers will also want to monitor the rate of engagement in their classrooms by measuring the number of OTRs students encounter. To ensure they are providing an adequate rate of OTRs, teachers can set an OTR rate goal and receive performance feedback by self-monitoring. Brandi Simonsen, Diane Myers, and Carla DeLuca (2010) found that when teachers received information about their daily rate of OTRs, they not only increased their rate of OTRs but also demonstrated more consistent use of OTRs. Additionally, research shows that when teachers set goals for implementing a strategy (for example, use of OTRs or praise statements) and then receive goal-related feedback, they are more likely to use the strategy (Cavanaugh, 2013).

Teachers can take three steps to monitor their use of OTRs in the classroom. First, determine a base rate—the starting frequency or rate of something prior to an intervention—of OTRs. As with behavior tracking, teachers can ask a colleague to conduct a ten-minute observation of a lesson and record the total number of OTRs using tally marks. Teachers can also video- or audio-record their own lessons and analyze them later. Take at least three collections of data and average the rates. "Monitoring Opportunities to Respond" (page 82) provides a template for conducting this step. After averaging the rates, compare the base rate of OTRs to the desired rate. Remember that the criterion for a desired OTR rate depends on the instructional format (whole-group or small-group instruction) and on how new the material is to students (see page 73). Use this comparison to set a goal for increasing the rate of OTRs. Next, identify instructional strategies to increase the rate of OTRs. Finally, re-evaluate your use of OTRs (through colleague observation or recording) and use this information to continue to adjust as necessary. Teachers can use "Analyzing OTR Data From Teacher Observations" (page 83) to set goals and track their rate of OTRs over time.

Summary

Active engagement is a manner of instruction in which students are provided ample opportunities to respond actively to instruction instead of sitting passively during lessons. In addition to improving academic outcomes, active engagement is an essential aspect of effective classroom management because students who are engaged in content are less likely to misbehave. Provide students with frequent opportunities to respond using verbal, written, or action response techniques. The foundation of classroom management covered thus far has involved creating and teaching expectations and rules, establishing procedures and structure in the classroom, reinforcing expectations, and ensuring high engagement among students. The final component of classroom management is to have an array of strategies to decrease and manage acts of misbehavior, which is the focus of the next chapter.

Chapter 5: Comprehension Questions

1. What are some benefits of active engagement?

2. What are the general types of student responses?

3. What is the difference between individual and choral responses?

4. What are the desired rates of OTRs for different types of instruction?

Monitoring Opportunities to Respond

Teacher: _____

Total Minutes of Observation: 10	Instructional Format:	
	☐ Introduction to new content ☐ Review of previously learned content	☐ Whole class ☐ Small group

	Day 1	Day 2	Day 3	Day 4	Day 5
Number of OTRs in the lesson (tallies):					
Total OTRs:					
Total OTRs ÷ 10 minutes = rate Rate per minute:					

My goal:	My base rate of OTRs is _____ per minute. My goal is to reach _____ OTRs per minute.

Strategies I will use to increase my rates of OTRs:	**Individual Responses** ☐ Cold calls ☐ Other: _____ ☐ Other: _____	**Choral Responses** ☐ Repetition ☐ Other: _____ ☐ Other: _____	**Peer-to-Peer Responses** ☐ Think-pair-share ☐ Classwide peer tutoring ☐ Other: _____
	Written Responses ☐ Whiteboards ☐ Guided notes ☐ Exit slips ☐ Text-related questions ☐ Other: _____	**Action Responses** ☐ Gestures ☐ Response cards ☐ Technology tools ☐ Other: _____	

Source: Adapted from Florida's Positive Behavior Support Project. (n.d.). Accessed at http://flpbs.fmhi.usf.edu/index.cfm on December 2, 2014. Also adapted from Partin, T. C., Robertson, R. E., Maggin, D. M., Oliver, R. M., & Wehby, J. H. (2010). Using teacher praise and opportunities to respond to promote appropriate student behavior. *Preventing School Failure, 54*(3), 172–178.

Analyzing OTR Data From Teacher Observations

Draw a horizontal line across the graph to represent the goal. Plot points on the graph each time an observation is conducted to indicate the average number of OTRs in each instructional session. Connect the points to show progress toward the goal.

Daily Rate of OTRs Per Minute

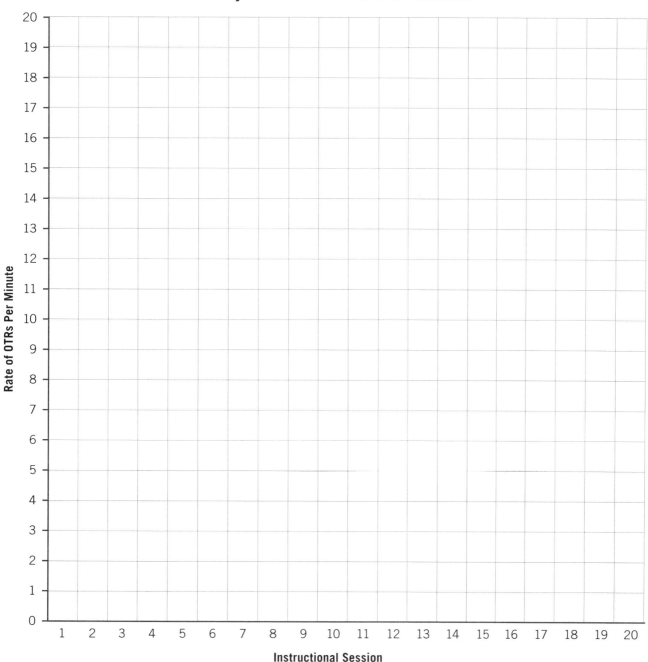

Instructional Session

Chapter 6

MANAGING MISBEHAVIOR

The final element of an effective classroom management plan is the use of a continuum of strategies to decrease unwanted behavior. In other words, the teacher has a variety of management strategies in place to prevent or deter students from behaving in a way that causes problems for others in the classroom. Managing misbehavior is not the same as punishing a student when he or she misbehaves. Instead, effective management involves reinforcing appropriate behavior and using instances of misbehavior as opportunities to teach more appropriate conduct (Alberto & Troutman, 2013; Carr et al., 2002; Wolery et al., 1988). Scott Stage and David Quiroz (1997) conducted a meta-analysis on different methods for managing disruptive behavior. The most effective methods involved reinforcement strategies (such as token economies) rather than punishment strategies (such as taking away privileges). Table 6.1 displays a summary of their findings; note that a negative effect size indicates a reduction of disruptive behavior—a desirable result in this case.

Table 6.1: Effect Sizes of Interventions on Disruptive Behavior

Intervention	Effect Size
Group Contingency	–1.02
Self-Management	–.97
Differential Reinforcement	–.95
Token Economies	–.90
Peer Management	–.79
Teacher Approval or Disapproval	–.77
Punishment	–.58
Response Cost	–.53
Functional Assessment	–.51
Cognitive-Behavioral Interventions	–.36
Individual Counseling	–.31

Source: Adapted from Stage & Quiroz, 1997.

As explored in chapter 1 (page 10), a key principle of effective classroom management is to teach students behavior in the same manner as academics. In the same way that a teacher does not punish a student for misreading a word or for incorrectly solving a math problem, teachers should try to first see misbehaviors as opportunities to teach appropriate conduct. This chapter describes the general process for managing misbehavior in the classroom. It does not, however, address persistent behavioral concerns of individual students; for information on responding to habitually disruptive behavior from specific students, see chapter 7 (page 99).

Types of Consequences

As discussed briefly in chapter 1 (page 8), there are two types of consequences: reinforcement and punishment (Skinner, 1953, 1976; Watson, 1913; see also Alberto & Troutman, 2013; Baer et al., 1968; Wolery et al., 1988). To review, reinforcement is a desirable outcome that increases the rate of a given behavior. Punishment is the opposite; it is an undesirable outcome that reduces the chance of a behavior occurring again in the future. Although the word *punishment* has negative connotations and is often used to refer to punitive penalties (such as removal of recess), it is strictly used here to refer to an outcome that reduces the chance of a behavior occurring again. Therefore, something can only be classified as a punishment if it actually decreases the rate of the behavior. Sometimes, a teacher or school applies a strategy that is meant to reduce rates of behavior (such as suspension or detention) but does not actually achieve that intent. Such a strategy, although aversive in nature, cannot accurately be classified as a punishment. The same logic applies for reinforcement. Although giving a student a sticker or reward may seem like reinforcement, it is only truly reinforcement if the desired behavior increases.

Teachers can use reinforcement and punishment in positive and negative ways. Here, the terms *positive* and *negative* are not synonyms for the terms *good* and *bad*. Rather, a positive consequence refers to the application of something, whereas a negative consequence refers to the removal of something. Therefore, there can be positive reinforcement, negative reinforcement, positive punishment, and negative punishment. Table 6.2 depicts the relationship of reinforcement and punishment to their positive and negative uses.

Table 6.2: The Positive and Negative Use of Consequences

	Positive (Adding Something)	Negative (Removing Something)
Reinforcement (Behavior Increases)	Adding something desirable (such as praise, a reward, a thumbs-up, and so on)	Removing something undesirable (such as reducing the length of an assignment)
Punishment (Behavior Decreases)	Adding something undesirable (such as a reprimand, extra homework, a detention, and so on)	Removing something desirable (such as taking away recess, taking away a minute from passing time between classes, and so on)

As shown in table 6.2, positive reinforcement causes a behavior to increase by adding something desirable (such as a ticket, token, prize, long-term reward, and so on). Negative reinforcement, on the other hand, causes a behavior to increase by removing something undesirable (such as allowing students to skip a number of problems on an assignment). Similarly, positive punishment causes a behavior to decrease by adding something undesirable (such as giving verbal reprimands), while negative punishment causes a behavior to decrease by removing something desirable (such as recess or computer time).

In response to undesirable behavior, teachers should begin with reinforcement rather than punishment. To illustrate, consider a seventh-grade student who frequently talks out of turn during class. To decrease this behavior, the teacher begins by adding verbal praise (positive reinforcement) every time the student performs a more desirable behavior, such as working quietly. If the student continues to call out, then the teacher uses punishment, such as scolding the student (a positive punishment) or taking away the student's recess privileges (a negative punishment). To regulate their use of reinforcement and punishment in response to misbehavior, teachers can use a management hierarchy.

The Management Hierarchy

In 2013, Paul Alberto and Anne Troutman described a four-level hierarchy for classroom management. Although their model focused on managing individual students' behavior, here it has been adapted for general classroom use. This adapted management hierarchy contains three levels.

1. **Reinforcement strategies:** The teacher applies strategies that reinforce or ensure use of the desired behavior (for example, increasing the rate of reinforcement a student receives or prompting students to use a certain behavior).

2. **Negative punishment:** The teacher removes desirable items or pleasant stimuli (for example, a student takes a time-out from a fun activity).

3. **Positive punishment:** The teacher applies unpleasant stimuli (for example, *overcorrection*, which is the repeated practice of a behavior designed to be aversive). Teachers should only use strategies within this level when documented efforts warrant their use.

Figure 6.1 depicts the arrangement of levels of the management hierarchy.

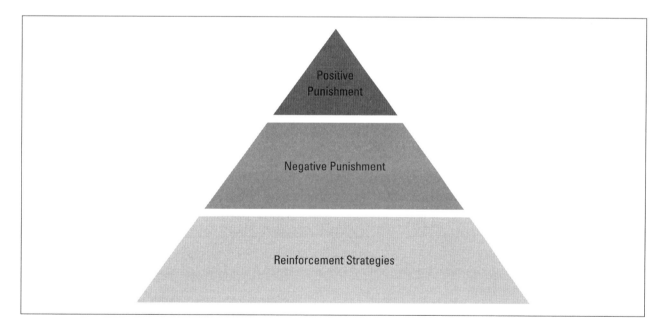

Figure 6.1: Levels of the management hierarchy.

The management hierarchy is built on three principles. First, begin with the least aversive and least intrusive strategies. The hierarchy is structured so that less intrusive, reinforcement-based strategies comprise the lower levels, and more aversive, punishment-based strategies are at higher levels. In response to misbehavior, teachers use the lower levels of the hierarchy first and only proceed up the hierarchy if the misbehavior persists. Second, the management hierarchy includes a focus on teaching appropriate replacement behaviors. If students are expected to refrain from a particular behavior, they should be taught an appropriate replacement behavior that serves the same purpose. Otherwise, they may return to the problem behavior because it served a purpose for them. Third, moving from one level of the category to the next requires the use of data. Decisions to use more aversive strategies should be based on documentation that less intrusive strategies have not been effective.

There are numerous strategies teachers can choose from at each level of the management hierarchy. Here, we describe the levels in more detail and suggest several practical strategies to implement for each. "Checklist of Management Strategies" (page 97) provides a checklist of these strategies to help teachers plan which ones they will use.

Level 1: Reinforcement Strategies

At level 1, a teacher encourages desirable behaviors through reinforcement strategies. These strategies include increased reinforcement, precorrection, active supervision, opportunities to practice, and error correction.

Increased Reinforcement

A simple first step for decreasing undesirable behavior is to provide more reinforcement for a desirable replacement behavior through the use of behavior-specific praise and short-term rewards. For example, if a student repeatedly calls out or leaves her seat during class, the teacher can watch for a desired replacement behavior (sitting quietly in her seat), praise the student for that behavior, and provide a short-term reward. Additionally, the teacher can examine the ratio of praise for the desired replacement behavior to redirect from the undesirable behavior and make adjustments to achieve the magic ratio of five instances of praise for every one redirect. This ensures that the student receives more attention for the desirable behavior than for the undesirable one.

Precorrection

Precorrection is proactive verbal prompting to prevent undesirable behaviors before they occur (Colvin, Sugai, & Patching, 1993). For example, a teacher might stand at the classroom door as students return from recess and remind them to enter the room silently for independent reading. Research has documented the benefit of precorrection—decreasing problematic behavior—in a variety of settings (Colvin et al., 1993; DePry & Sugai, 2002; Ennis, Schwab, & Jolivette, 2012; Lampi, Fenty, & Beaunae, 2005; Lewis, Colvin, & Sugai, 2000; Simonsen et al., 2008; Stormont et al., 2007). Although precorrection typically involves verbal prompting, teachers can use other prompts as well. Table 6.3 lists examples of three types of prompts: (1) verbal, (2) visual, (3) and physical.

As shown in table 6.3, teachers can use verbal, visual, or physical prompts to help set students up for success. Teachers should follow these steps when precorrecting behavior:

1. Determine when and where problem behaviors occur and what triggers them (using observation data).

2. Identify appropriate replacement behaviors.

3. Conduct behavior rehearsals, teaching and practicing the replacement behavior in context so students understand how to perform it accurately.

4. Provide strong positive reinforcement for the replacement behavior when students perform it.

5. In context, prompt the replacement behavior (verbally, visually, or physically), monitor students' performance, and correct as needed.

Using precorrection to simply remind students of behavioral expectations can help prevent misbehavior before it occurs.

Table 6.3: Examples for Three Types of Prompts

Type	Example
Verbal	Remind students of the expectations before an event occurs.
	Ask a student to share the expectations or have each student share with a partner.
	Ask students to think of an expectation they might follow during the next event.
Visual	Post rules on the classroom walls.
	Post pictures of gestures that indicate certain expectations, such as a picture of eyes and ears to remind students to "Look and listen."
	Point to a color on a poster to show the level of noise that is appropriate for the activity (red = no voices, yellow = quiet voices, green = normal voices).
Physical	Gently move a student by the shoulders into a line before the class starts moving down the hall.
	Place tape on the floor to indicate boundaries for each section of the classroom.
	Turn off the lights before students enter the classroom after lunch to indicate that it is time to quiet down.

Source: Adapted from Colvin et al., 1993.

Active Supervision

Active supervision involves three steps: (1) scan the classroom, (2) identify instances of desirable behavior, and (3) praise the student(s) performing the behavior (privately or in front of the class). Active supervision has been shown to reduce rates of misbehavior in classrooms (DePry & Sugai, 2002), as well as in unstructured settings such as the playground or cafeteria (Lewis et al., 2000). Randall DePry and George Sugai (2002) demonstrated the effectiveness of precorrection and active supervision within a sixth-grade general education classroom. The rate of minor misbehavior in the classroom dropped from 90 percent to less than 65 percent during the first implementation of the intervention and to less than 40 percent at the second implementation.

Opportunities to Practice

When students consistently demonstrate an undesirable behavior, teachers can respond by simply reteaching the desirable replacement behavior and providing opportunities to practice. First, model and teach the replacement behavior. Next, have students perform the replacement behavior in a safe setting; that is, do not punish the students for committing errors. Once the students can perform the replacement behavior well, ask them to perform it in real-life situations. For example, students can practice lining up at the door in a role-play scenario before actually lining up at the door for recess. Finally, provide students with feedback on their performance with the replacement behavior. *Performance feedback* is data that indicate whether a person is performing a particular desired behavior (Balcazar, Hopkins,

& Suarez, 1986). Such feedback can help students modify their behavior in the same way it can help adults (for example, consider road signs that detect and digitally display the speeds of passing cars beside the posted speed limit).

Error Correction

When a student performs an undesirable or unwanted behavior, the teacher can engage in *error correction* by modeling or reminding the student of the corresponding correct behavior and asking the student to try again (Kame'enui & Simmons, 1990; Watkins & Slocum, 2004). For example, if a student exclaims, "I'm done!" to indicate that he has finished an assignment, begin by acknowledging the student. Next, explain the correct behavior (such as quietly turning in the assignment), model it, and ask the student to perform it correctly. Praise the student for performing the correct behavior and move on in the lesson. This process is depicted in table 6.4.

Table 6.4: Procedure for Error Corrections

Step	Examples
1. An incorrect behavior occurs.	A student talks out of turn in class. A student disrupts the class by running up to an adult who has entered the room.
2. Identify the corresponding correct behavior or offer an appropriate replacement behavior.	The teacher says, "Remember, we raise our hands because it respectfully signals to others that we would like to make a comment." The teacher says, "When a visitor comes into class, students wave silently from their desks to say hello."
3. If necessary, model the behavior to the student.	The teacher raises her hand. The teacher waves silently with one finger over her lips.
4. Ask the student to perform the correct behavior.	The teacher says, "Try it again, but this time, raise your hand." The teacher says, "Let's try that again. I'm going to ask Mr. Davis to leave the room and come back in. When he comes back in, wave from your desks."
5. Praise or reinforce and thank the student for compliance.	The teacher says, "Thank you for being respectful by raising your hand! How can I help you?" "Yes! That's how we greet visitors. Thank you for doing it correctly."

As mentioned earlier, misbehavior provides an opportunity to reteach. For example, a teacher might ask a student who runs down the hallway to stop, go back, and walk. In this situation, the student knows the skill (walking) and can perform it, so modeling is not necessary. On the other hand, if a student tells a peer, "Get out of my way!" while lining up, a teacher might model some more appropriate ways to request more personal space—a replacement behavior—and then ask the student to perform the new behavior. When used effectively, error correction is quick and efficient, gives the student a chance to try again, and ends with praise and reinforcement.

Level 2: Negative Punishment

If strategies at level 1 of the management hierarchy are not effective at replacing undesirable behaviors with desirable behaviors, the teacher moves to level 2: negative punishment. Negative punishment involves taking something desirable away from the student. Teachers can provide negative punishment to students in three ways: (1) extinction, (2) loss of privileges, or (3) a time-out from reinforcement.

Extinction

Extinction is the process of withholding reinforcement for a certain problem behavior (Skinner, 1953; Wolery et al., 1988). The idea behind extinction is that when a behavior that was previously reinforced is no longer reinforced, that behavior will no longer be used by the student. Because the behavior no longer earns reinforcement, the behavior is no longer useful and a different behavior will be used. Extinction is commonly used with students who call out in class to get the teacher's attention. To use extinction with this problem behavior, the teacher stops responding to it and instead requires that the student use a new behavior (for example, raising his or her hand) to get the teacher's attention. That is, the teacher does not respond to a student who calls out and only acknowledges or answers the student when he or she uses the appropriate replacement behavior. In this way, extinction is often paired with reinforcement of an appropriate behavior in order to facilitate the acquisition of a new behavior. Thus, attention (which is what the student wants) is contingent upon using the new replacement behavior, and the problem behavior is no longer effective.

Loss of Privileges

A simple negative punishment a teacher can apply at level 2 is the removal of desirable activities or privileges, such as trips outside for recess or attendance at school events. Fay and Funk (1995) stressed that teachers should be sure to logically tie the removal of privileges to a specific behavior. For example, a student who behaves aggressively during recess might lose access to future recess time. If the behavior occurred outside of recess time, it makes less logical sense to remove the student's recess privileges.

Time-Out From Reinforcement

In a time-out from reinforcement, the teacher denies the student access to all forms of reinforcement for a set amount of time. Teachers can use four different types of time-outs, depending on the needs of the student or the severity of the situation (Ryan, Sanders, Katsiyannis, & Yell, 2007; Wolery et al., 1988):

1. **Nonseclusionary time-out**—Students stay in the classroom, but they are excluded from certain reinforcing activities or tasks. For example, a student may put his or her head down on his or her desk or sit silently for a few minutes during a class game. Some teachers have all students wear ribbons, badges, or wristbands. If a student displays unwanted behavior, the teacher removes the ribbon to signify that the student has started a period of time-out.

2. **Contingent observation**—The student moves to a different part of the classroom but can still observe the activity. Some teachers call this area the "penalty box" or the "cool down chair."

3. **Exclusionary time-out**—The teacher moves the student away from the activity (such as to another classroom). In a contingent observation, the student can still observe the activity, but in an exclusionary time-out, the student can neither observe nor participate.

4. **Seclusionary time-out**—The teacher isolates the student in a designated time-out room. This is the most restrictive form of time-out and should be reserved for situations that involve physical aggression, severe verbal aggression, or destruction of property. Because schools must consider legal and ethical matters when using seclusionary time-outs, teachers should not use them without the support of a district or administrative team.

When using time-outs, keep a few guiding principles in mind. For one, take care not to use time-outs with students who are trying to escape an activity or instruction. A student who refuses to complete an assignment, for example, might find a time-out reinforcing because he or she wanted to avoid work in the first place. Keep the time-out area separate from potential reinforcement (for example, do not put a student in the hallway for time-out if other students may be passing by). Additionally, clarify the kinds of behavior that warrant a time-out, how a time-out ends, and how long it lasts (whether it lasts for a fixed amount of time or whether it lasts until the student displays the appropriate behavior). Practice the proper time-out procedure before any student earns one. Monitor your own use of time-outs; avoid giving time-outs to students just to get a break from them. "Matrix for Planning Classroom Time-Outs" (page 98) provides a template to assist teachers with appropriate time-outs. Finally, include a debriefing session after the time-out to help the student reflect on why he or she earned a time-out, and figure out what to do differently next time.

A *debrief* facilitates a student's transition from a time-out back to the normal routine. George Sugai and Geoffrey Colvin (1997) stated that during a debrief, the student briefly reflects on the events that triggered the problem behavior (for example, "I was frustrated with my seatwork"), identifies future expected behaviors ("Next time, I should ask for help"), and expresses preparedness to return to the classroom or instructional setting ("I'm ready to go back to class now"). Debriefing should last only a few minutes. Do not use this time to lecture the student. Instead, help the student identify and practice a replacement behavior, and prepare him or her to resume the day as usual. A student might complete a form or answer questions verbally during the debriefing process. Figure 6.2 presents a sample reflection form for a debriefing session.

Name: Date:	
What happened?	
Where, when, and why did the problem behavior occur?	
What will you do next time instead of using a problem behavior?	
What do you need to do after you complete this form?	
Do you need help after you complete this form?	

Figure 6.2: Sample reflection form to use during debriefing.

Source: Adapted from Sugai & Colvin, 1997.

Level 3: Positive Punishment

The final level of the management hierarchy involves positive punishment, or the application of undesirable consequences. Positive punishment never includes causing physical harm to a student or threatening a student's safety. Instead, positive punishment involves the application of mildly aversive tasks or situations. Students who continually litter at lunch, for example, may receive the chore of cleaning up the entire cafeteria. A student who has continually behaved in an unsafe way in the classroom may be required to write a detailed apology to each student in the class.

Teachers should reserve the strategies presented at level 3 for use only as a last resort. As explained previously, only use strategies at level 3 when prior, documented attempts have not reduced the problematic behavior. Teachers should keep two important considerations in mind when using strategies at level 3. First, whenever possible, a student's parents or guardians should be aware of the use of positive punishment and should agree to any strategy before it is implemented. Second, positive punishment should only be used to the extent necessary. Once the misbehavior decreases, remove the positive punishment. Strategies at level 3 include overcorrection and use of apology letters.

Overcorrection

Overcorrection (Foxx & Bechtel, 1982) involves having a student perform an appropriate behavior to a greater degree than might ordinarily be warranted by a particular misbehavior. For example, a student who repeatedly writes on his or her desk might be required to clean *all* the desks in a classroom.

Teachers can use two forms of overcorrection: resititutional and positive practice. *Restitutional* overcorrection requires that a student restore the appearance or cleanliness of a setting (such as a classroom, cafeteria, and so on) above and beyond its original condition. For example, a student might clean an entire classroom after continuously throwing paper on the floor. In *positive practice* overcorrection, the student performs the correct behavior in a repeated and exaggerated way. This differs from error correction (see page 90) in that the student does not simply perform the correct behavior once or twice, but many times. For example, a student who consistently runs down the hallway may eventually be asked to walk back and forth several times down the hall as a form of overcorrection. A class that struggles with lining up may practice lining up and sitting down several times in a row.

Before using overcorrection, note that it requires continual monitoring from a teacher. Because this requires the teacher's full attention, overcorrection can be very time consuming. As with previous strategies, keep punishment from becoming arbitrary or vindictive by ensuring that it logically fits the misbehavior (for example, the student cleans up the same room where he or she threw paper on the floor or walks down the same hall that he or she ran down). Guide students through each step of the overcorrection to ensure accurate performance, and adjust guidance as the student performs the behavior (Foxx & Bechtel, 1982).

Apology Letters

Another example of positive punishment is the use of apology letters or written notes to those affected by students' misbehavior (White & White, 1990). For example, a class that is disruptive and noisy can write letters to other classrooms or students they disrupted. Although the act of writing apology letters should be somewhat aversive in order to qualify as a positive punishment strategy, the letters should consist of genuine communication and focus on clarity. For example, if two students argued, both parties would sit down and write letters to each other describing what happened. They would then exchange their letters and write rebuttals. This process should lead to a resolution or agreement to avoid future instances of the initial problem behavior (White & White, 1990).

Tracking Misbehavior

As explained previously, teachers should record instances of misbehavior in the classroom and use the data to support decisions about movement up the management hierarchy. A simple way to record behavior data is to use behavior tracking slips to document the occurrence of the problem behavior. This tracking tool records instances of problem behavior so teachers can identify patterns in the types, locations, and times of behavioral issues, as well as the students involved (Colvin, 2007; George et al., 2009). Within a classroom, the tracking form can be an individual slip of paper for each incident (see figure 6.3) or a table in which the teacher tallies instances of specific behaviors by student (see figure 6.4).

Student: _____

Date: _____   **Time:** _____

Behavior (Mark one):

_____ Disruption

_____ Defiance

_____ Disrespect

_____ Academic dishonesty

_____ Invasion of personal space

_____ Inappropriate language

_____ Damage to school property

_____ Property misuse

_____ Technology violation

_____ Other: _____

Where:

_____ Classroom

_____ Hallway

_____ Other: _____

Figure 6.3: Example of an individual behavior tracking sheet.

Source: Adapted from Colvin, 2007.

To use individual behavior slips like the one in figure 6.3, the teacher should create a small form (perhaps a quarter-sheet of paper) that lists various types of problem behavior to be checked off or circled and includes space to record the student's name, the date and time of the incident, and the location where it occurred. The teacher keeps a stack of these slips on his or her desk and quickly fills one out each time a problematic behavior occurs. Later, the teacher can review the completed forms to identify patterns.

With a classwide behavior tracking form (such as figure 6.4), teachers simply add tally marks to the table to indicate instances of a specific behavior by a specific student. The classwide table is quick and easy to fill out, even during lessons, and provides data on which behaviors are most problematic for a whole class or particular student; however, it does not identify locations or difficult times of day.

	Students				
	Aaron	**Paul**	**Jessie**	**Jamie**	**Abby**
Disruption					
Defiance					
Disrespect					
Academic Dishonesty					
Inappropriate Language					
Property Misuse					

Figure 6.4: Example of a classwide behavior tracking form.

Summary

As part of an effective classroom management system, teachers use a management hierarchy to manage misbehavior. The first level consists of nonaversive reinforcement strategies, which are used prior to the second and third levels—negative punishment and positive punishment, respectively. If the less aversive methods are not successful, then the decision to use more aversive methods should be based on classroom behavior data. This hierarchy of strategies is useful for managing misbehavior for the entire classroom. However, there are times when general classroom management is an insufficient response to the behavior of certain students. The next chapter provides direction on managing more challenging individual student behavior.

Chapter 6: Comprehension Questions

1. What is the difference between reinforcement and punishment?

2. What do the terms *negative* and *positive* mean in the context of behavior management? What do negative and positive reinforcement and punishment look like in practice?

3. How can reinforcement be used to decrease problem behavior?

4. Explain the reasoning behind the order of the management hierarchy.

Checklist of Management Strategies

Identify the strategies you will use for each level of the management hierarchy. Mark a check by the listed strategy or write your own within the box.

Level 1 Reinforcement Strategies	Level 2 Negative Punishment	Level 3 Positive Punishment
☐ Increased Reinforcement ☐ Precorrection ☐ Active Supervision ☐ Opportunities to Practice ☐ Error Correction ☐ Other: _____	☐ Extinction ☐ Loss of Privileges ☐ Time-Out From Reinforcement ☐ Other: _____	☐ Overcorrection ☐ Apology Letters ☐ Other: _____

Matrix for Planning Classroom Time-Outs

	Nonseclusionary Time-Outs	Contingent Observations	Exclusionary Time-Outs
Description			
Examples			
What behaviors earn a time-out?			
Where will it take place?			
Will students receive a warning before a time-out?			
How long will the time-out last?			
What activities will students do during a time-out?			
Who will supervise?			
How does a time-out end?			
What is the debriefing process?			

Chapter 7

PROVIDING INDIVIDUALIZED BEHAVIOR SUPPORT

The previous chapters in this book have outlined the elements of a proactive, instructional behavior management plan for classrooms. However, certain students require more individualized attention. This chapter outlines general guidelines for approaching individualized behavior plans. First, we discuss a few considerations for working with students who demonstrate noncompliant behavior. Next, we provide a broad process for developing individual plans and interventions for students, including information on function-based support and the escalation cycle.

Noncompliance

Noncompliant students do not follow directions or comply with teacher requests (Alter, Walker, & Landers, 2013; Ingersoll & Smith, 2003; Little, 2005). To respond to noncompliance, teachers can use three general strategies: (1) precision commands, (2) behavioral momentum, and (3) instructional choice. Here, we describe each of these strategies.

Precision Commands

Precision commands are sequences of responses used when providing directions to noncompliant students (Mackay, McLaughlin, Weber, & Derby, 2001). Namely, when a teacher gives an instruction, the student has roughly ten seconds to comply. If the student complies, the teacher provides reinforcement (behavior-specific praise and a short-term reward). If the student does not comply within this time frame, the teacher addresses the student, makes a more direct request (for example, "Jackie, I need you to sit down in your seat"), and waits another ten seconds, providing reinforcement if the student complies. If the student still has not followed instructions after this second request, the teacher gives a preplanned consequence for noncompliance. Figure 7.1 (page 100) depicts this sequence of precision commands and reinforcements in the form of a flow chart. The preplanned consequence may either be part of the management hierarchy (page 87) or part of an individually designed behavior plan for the student. For example, if the student has reached level 2 in the hierarchy, he or she receives a two-minute time-out for noncompliance. If the student has reached level 3, the teacher might use an overcorrection procedure.

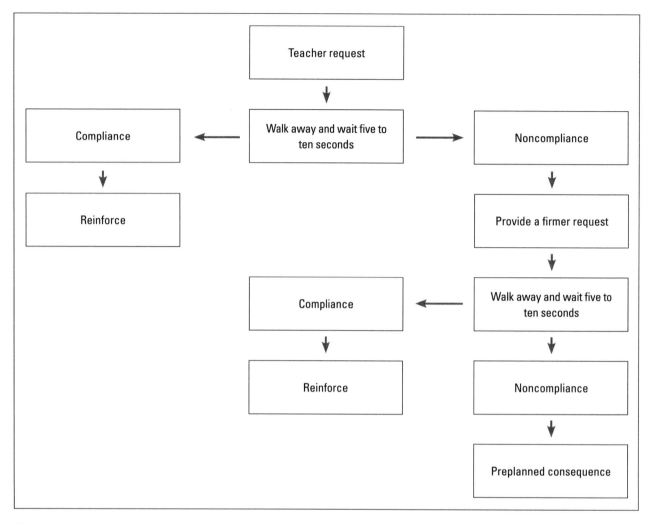

Figure 7.1: Sequence of precision commands and reinforcements.

Keep in mind that students can interpret instructions differently depending on how a teacher phrases them. For example, instructions that use vague language, include numerous requests, or are phrased in the form of a question (such as "Can't you ever walk down the hallway? You're always running!")—called *beta commands* by Rex Forehand and Robert McMahon (1981)—can confuse or frustrate students. Beta commands also make it more difficult for a teacher to discern why a student has not followed instructions. It is possible that the student is choosing to misbehave, but it is also possible that the student simply does not understand the instructions the teacher has given. To avoid this ambiguity, teachers should use *alpha commands*—clear, concise, and behavior-specific instructions—such as "Walk down the hall instead of running." Table 7.1 presents examples of both alpha and beta commands.

Distinguishing between alpha and beta commands can help a teacher determine whether a student is choosing not to follow directions or is simply missing a behavioral skill and requires reteaching (Gresham, 2002; VanDerHeyden & Witt, 2008). Reflect on the phrasing of the instruction and assess whether it can be made more explicit. For instance, if a student is expected to line up but has trouble keeping his hands to himself, the teacher might break down the instruction to line up into more explicit steps (such as "Stand up, push in your chair, fold your arms across your chest, and walk toward the line when called").

Table 7.1: Sample Alpha and Beta Commands

Alpha	Beta
I want you to finish your lunch as soon as possible.	Why are you still eating? Hurry up.
Show me what you have completed so far.	Have you completed any work? You need to finish.
Put away your book and papers.	Clean up your mess.
Stand right here and wait for your classmates.	Straighten up.
Write your name on the paper as soon as you get it.	Don't you remember what to do when you get your paper? I always have to remind you.

After the teacher provides more explicit instructions and assesses the student's knowledge of the skill, he or she may suspect that the student is choosing not to comply in spite of having the ability to do so. To further assess a student's ability to perform a skill, a teacher can ask the student to practice the skill in a safe setting (without other students in the room). If the student performs the skill accurately, the student is probably choosing not to perform it in a given setting. Additionally, teachers can conduct assessments in which they offer rewards to students to perform the skill. Students who perform behaviors properly if given an incentive probably do not need reteaching, but do need more motivation and practice to perform the skill. In this case, teachers can manipulate antecedents and consequences, as well as provide the student with more time to practice the skill in various settings (Gresham, 2002; VanDerHeyden & Witt, 2008).

Behavioral Momentum

Teachers can proactively mitigate noncompliance by providing smaller, easier instructions to a student before providing more difficult or time-intensive ones. This process can help ease students into following directions. F. Charles Mace and his colleagues (1988) referred to this technique as establishing *behavioral momentum*. A teacher creates behavioral momentum when he or she provides a high-probability request (that is, a request with which the student is likely to comply and that is not difficult to perform) prior to providing a low-probability request (that is, a request with which the student is less likely to comply). For example, a teacher can preface an instruction to complete a worksheet by first asking the student to sit in his or her seat, then to take out a pencil, and then to write his or her name on the worksheet.

For students with a history of noncompliance, school can be a situation in which their interactions are often negative and consist of multiple tasks that may be difficult to complete because of missing skills. This can lead to limited praise or acknowledgment (Sutherland & Wehby, 2001). Consequently, many of their experiences at school may be unpleasant and their access to reinforcement (for example, praise, completion of tasks, and so on) may be considerably more limited than students who do not have a history of noncompliance. By using behavioral momentum, teachers can create multiple positive interactions with students before asking them to perform a difficult task. Students are given directions with which they are likely to comply, thus creating momentum with compliance and access to reinforcement (that is, praise for compliance and positive social interactions with the teacher). Once momentum is established with a few easy requests, a lower-probability request can be made. For example, a student may be noncompliant when asked to complete longer, more difficult math problems. Her teacher could use behavioral momentum by asking her to complete small, high-probability tasks, such as writing her name on the paper, sharpening a pencil, and completing easier problems before asking her to complete a more difficult problem. The teacher could also intersperse easier problems throughout the assignment in order to maintain compliance. By completing smaller tasks, the student receives reinforcement prior to being asked to perform a task he or she does not necessarily enjoy.

Instructional Choice

Providing students with a measure of academic choice can also help teachers respond to noncompliance. *Instructional choice* involves presenting a student with two or more alternatives from a teacher-developed menu (Hoffman & DuPaul, 2000; Walker, 1997). In this strategy, the teacher typically allows the student to choose between two academic activities (such as silent reading or silent writing) or to choose the order of activities (for example, reading first and then writing). For example, a teacher may say to a student, "Alec, the class is now working on independent seat work. You have a choice of what you want to work on. You can complete your vocabulary cards or work on your reading questions. Which would you like to do?" This option helps students transition back into compliant behavior by engaging in a preferred activity.

Using Individualized Behavior Plans

As previously explained, an *individualized behavior plan* is an intervention that is designed to manage the behavior of a specific student. Some students require a very detailed plan to correct certain problematic behavior. While the help of an expert in the school (such as a school psychologist or counselor) is often needed to create and implement an individualized behavior plan, a teacher can sometimes provide support independently if the issue is relatively minor or has not grown too large to manage alone. Teachers can refer to the following four steps when creating individualized behavior plans:

1. Clearly define the problematic behavior.

2. Determine the function of the behavior.

3. Design an intervention to target the behavior.

4. Monitor and track the intervention's effectiveness.

The following sections describe each step.

Clearly Define the Problematic Behavior

Before implementing an individualized behavior plan, the teacher must define the behavior in observable and measurable terms, clearly describing what the behavior looks and sounds like. The teacher should precisely define the frequency, intensity, and characteristics of the behavior to the extent that if a stranger read the definition, he or she could immediately identify the behavior (Alberto & Troutman, 2013). For example, rather than saying that a student "throws a fit," which is vague and might look different for different students, a teacher should say that the student "pounds his fists on the desk and yells." This step allows the teacher to hone in on the behavior that requires correction and avoid ambiguity in later steps of the plan. If more than one behavior requires correction, the teacher should take the time to parse out and clearly define each one before proceeding to intervention.

Determine the Function of the Behavior

To figure out the best intervention to use, the teacher must determine the function of the problem behavior so he or she will be able to identify a replacement behavior that matches the function of the original problem behavior (Crone & Horner, 2003). In this sense, function refers to the purpose of the behavior. For example, one student may perform a problem behavior to escape difficult work (the function of the problem behavior is to get away from something), whereas another may use a problem behavior to gain access to a peer (the function of the behavior is to get peer attention). Determining the function can involve a functional behavior assessment, which is usually conducted by a school psychologist. However, a classroom teacher can still make an informed guess about the function of the student's behavior. Specifically, teachers can examine existing data or collect their own data to determine a behavior's function.

First, a teacher could examine existing data on the student's behavior, perhaps from office discipline referrals. Office referrals often indicate the presumed function of a student's behavior, so a teacher could use this data to identify which behaviors the student is performing most often for a specific purpose. Otherwise, a teacher could collect his or her own data on the function of the student's behavior, either in one day or over the course of several days. To track the presumed function of the behavior, it is necessary to first define the behavior in clear, observable, and measurable terms. Then, create a checklist of possible functions of the behavior.

Teachers may gather information on potential antecedents as well. Throughout the day, mark each instance of behavior, as well as the corresponding antecedents and consequences, and assess the data to identify a pattern. As discussed in chapter 1, an antecedent is the act, incident, or condition that triggers a behavior and a consequence is an event or response that influences the probability of the behavior happening again. Teachers can use "Antecedent and Consequence Tracking Form" (page 113) to mark events that occur prior to the behavior (in the antecedent column) and events that occur after the behavior (in the consequences column). By examining patterns of antecedents, behaviors, and consequences, teachers can identify the most likely functions of a behavior. Alternatively, a different staff member can interview the teacher, student, or both, and then complete a survey or questionnaire. "Behavior Assessment Interview" (pages 114–116)provides an example of a brief interview that can be used.

Design an Intervention to Target the Behavior

Once a teacher has determined the probable function of the student's behavior, he or she can design an intervention. The intervention is meant to teach the student a replacement behavior that serves the same function as the problematic behavior. For example, if the student uses misbehavior to obtain adult attention (such as calling out or arguing), the teacher might offer the student some different, more appropriate ways to obtain attention, such as raising his or her hand or saying "Excuse me" before starting a conversation. If the student uses misbehavior to avoid work (for example, the student gets up from his or her seat and wanders around the classroom disrupting other students), a teacher can teach a more appropriate behavior that allows for a break from work—such as providing the student with a pass for a five-minute break—while also ensuring the student has the necessary skills to complete the work in the first place.

In designing an intervention, a teacher should consider the three points of intervention presented in chapter 1 (page 7; Bambara & Kern, 2005; Crone & Horner, 2003):

1. **Antecedent strategies**—The teacher prevents or avoids a behavior by adjusting the antecedent that triggers the behavior.

2. **Behavior strategies**—The teacher informs the student of a more efficient and effective replacement behavior.

3. **Consequence strategies**—The teacher reinforces the replacement behavior while putting the unwanted behavior on extinction or decreasing the unwanted behavior with punishment.

Select strategies that target antecedents, behaviors, and consequences. Although teachers always intervene at the behavior stage by teaching a replacement behavior, there are many different ways to intervene at the antecedent and consequence stages. Table 7.2 displays examples of common antecedent and consequence interventions.

Table 7.2: Sample Strategies for Intervening at the Antecedent and Consequence Strategies

Antecedent Strategies	Consequence Strategies
• Adjust work so it does not trigger avoidance behavior. • Provide a daily schedule to increase structure and awareness. • Provide instructional choice when introducing work. • Adjust the seating arrangements or schedule. • Enlist the help of peers or aides to provide prompts and reminders.	• Place problem behavior on extinction. • Provide a temporary plan to heavily reinforce new behavior. • Provide performance feedback. • Provide various types of reinforcement for the new behavior (for example, verbal, social, or tangible). • Use differential reinforcement.

One consequence intervention warrants a brief explanation: *differential reinforcement* (Alberto & Troutman, 2013; Deitz & Repp, 1973, 1983; Wolery et al., 1988). This strategy involves providing reinforcement for a particular behavior in ways that act as gradual steps to help a struggling student display more appropriate behavior. A teacher might provide differential reinforcement for a student displaying lower rates of the problem behavior, even if the behavior is not completely eliminated. For example, consider a student who takes ten minutes to transition from one activity to another. The transition period ideally takes two or three minutes; however, it may be too difficult for the student who takes ten minutes to suddenly complete the transition in fewer than three minutes, so the teacher provides differential reinforcement when the student transitions in six minutes. A teacher could also differentially reinforce a student's behavior over a set period of time. Instead of expecting that a typically disruptive student stay quiet all day, the teacher might reward the student if he goes thirty minutes without speaking out of turn. Differential reinforcement also comes into play when teachers reinforce the replacement behavior. In sum, differential reinforcement serves as a stepping stone to appropriate behavior.

As stated previously, intervention plans should consider antecedent, behavior, and consequence strategies, as well as evaluation procedures to measure their effectiveness (Newton, Horner, Todd, Algozzine, & Algozzine, 2012). "Intervention Design Template" (page 117) provides a template for designing an effective intervention. As an illustration of this process, consider figures 7.2 and 7.3 (pages 105–106), which detail an example problem behavior and the corresponding intervention. This example may be familiar to many teachers—a student who talks and is off task during independent work time. In this example, talking to peers (behavior) is triggered by the start of seat work when students are expected to work independently and quietly (antecedent). The behavior of talking to peers and not completing work is reinforced by the attention received from peers (consequence). Although some students may misbehave to avoid work, this example illustrates a student who performs a behavior to gain peer attention. If the function of the unwanted behavior (talking to peers) was to avoid work, the intervention would be different (for example, it might focus on teaching new academic skills). It is important to match the function of the behavior to the appropriate intervention in order to create an effective intervention plan (Dunlap et al., 2005).

Antecedent	Behavior	Consequence
Students are given independent seat work.	The student turns and talks to peers or wanders over to peers' desks. The student makes negative comments or interrupts peers.	The student obtains peer interaction (the student's behavior is reinforced by peer attention).

Figure 7.2: Example of problem behavior.

Point of Intervention	Component	Description	Example
Antecedent	Prevention	Implement strategies that minimize or prevent the occurrence of the behavior by modifying the antecedent.	• Provide appropriate time for student interaction before starting work. • Provide a precorrection. • Give the student a job to pass out papers, during which he can positively interact with others.
Behavior	Teaching	Teach a new behavior that replaces the old behavior and serves the same function.	• Reteach expectations for seat work. • Teach social skills so the student can gain peer attention appropriately and at appropriate times. • Teach the student to complete work instead of seeking peer attention (and to seek peer attention at appropriate times).
Consequence	Reinforcement	Praise and reinforce the new behavior.	• If the student completes work and does not interrupt peers, he can tell an appropriate joke or make an announcement to the class. • Praise the student when he follows expectations and uses appropriate social skills.
	Extinction and Punishment	Stop reinforcing the old behavior (extinction) and implement punishment strategies, including procedures that ensure the old behavior is not reinforced.	Level 1: Reteach and reinforce appropriate peer interaction at the appropriate time. Provide opportunities to interact with peers (for example, pair the student with a classmate and provide an organized activity to do during recess). Level 2: Have peers ignore the student or remind the student to return to his or her desk. Give the student a time-out in the hallway away from peers. Level 3: Have the student introduce himself or herself in an exaggerated fashion to every student in the classroom at an appropriate time.

Figure 7.3: Example of an intervention.

Continued on next page →

Point of Intervention	Component	Description	Example
Evaluation	Evaluation of Fidelity	Design a simple, efficient way to measure the fidelity of the plan, or the extent to which the intervention is implemented as intended.	• Document whether expectations were retaught and new social skills were taught. • Document whether the student obtains peer attention at appropriate times. • Document whether student uses new skills.
	Evaluation of Effectiveness	Design a simple, efficient way to measure the effectiveness of the plan.	• Observe and take note of the number of times the student gets out of his or her seat. • Monitor the amount of work the student completes.

Source: Adapted from Newton et al., 2012.

When the class is given independent seat work, the student uses inappropriate behavior to obtain attention from peers. The teacher addresses this by teaching the student appropriate ways to seek peer attention (that is, positive social skills) and to seek peer attention at appropriate times. Antecedent strategies include providing peer attention prior to seat work and reminding the student of appropriate expectations during seat work. Consequence strategies include reinforcement when the student behaves appropriately and punishment in accordance with the management hierarchy if the misbehavior continues. The intervention plan also includes strategies for evaluating its success.

Monitor and Track the Intervention's Effectiveness

Once an intervention plan is developed and implemented, it is important to collect data to determine how well the intervention is working. Although an exhaustive discussion of measuring behavior and collecting data is beyond the scope of this chapter (for more information, see Alberto & Troutman, 2013; Bambara & Kern, 2005; Steege & Watson, 2009), generally speaking, educators can either directly or indirectly document the behavior of interest (Whitcomb & Merrell, 2012). Direct measures of behavior involve observing the behavior and recording the instance when the behavior occurs (for example, making tally marks on a data sheet during class each time a student talks out of turn, or periodically checking for the behavior at predetermined intervals; Alberto & Troutman, 2013; Whitcomb & Merrell, 2012), or documenting occurrences shortly after they occur (for example, marking down the number of times a student talked out of turn when class ends). Indirect measures of behavior involve tracking the behavior without directly observing it (Kerr & Nelson, 2006; Miltenberger, 2005). For example, interviews with those who work closely with the student (such as parents or other school staff) are useful to determine the rate of behavior. The teacher can also examine the student's work to determine if he or she was off task during class (the idea being that if the student was disruptive, he or she wouldn't be able to complete his or her work). The previous chapter briefly discussed several methods for tracking behavior (see pages 94–95). Additionally, teachers may consider consulting with a behavior expert, such as the school psychologist, social worker, or counselor, to determine the best way to monitor a student's behavior.

The Escalation Cycle

Even the most complete and effective classroom management system or individualized intervention cannot prevent all incidents of misbehavior. At some point in their careers, most teachers face incidents that escalate quickly or deal with students who react with aggressive outbursts. Although such incidents can be difficult and even frightening to address, these explosive responses do follow a fairly predictable pattern (Colvin, 2004). Developing awareness of this pattern can help teachers proactively intervene before the student melts down. Geoff Colvin (2004), who referred to this pattern as the *escalation cycle*, described seven distinct phases in the process:

1. Calm

2. Trigger

3. Agitation

4. Acceleration

5. Peak

6. De-Escalation

7. Recovery

Table 7.3 describes these phases.

Table 7.3: Student Behaviors and Ideal Teacher Responses During the Escalation Cycle

Phase	Student Behavior	Teacher Response
Calm	Cooperative and responsive to directions	Effective classroom management
Trigger	Experiences unresolved conflict, inciting incident, or gradual buildup of negative events	Precorrection and formal problem solving (such as curriculum changes or teaching new skills)
Agitation	Unfocused, agitated, or anxious	Provision of personal space and allowance of preferred activities
Acceleration	Intense behavior meant to elicit a response	Calm, direct, and disengaged demeanor; provision of choice; and avoidance of negative interaction
Peak	Aggressive or unsafe	Isolation or removal of student from the classroom
De-Escalation	Unfocused and confused	Provision of time to calm down and complete independent work
Recovery	Agitated, subdued, or cooperative	Problem-solving to identify replacement behaviors and new skills

Source: Adapted from Colvin, 2004.

The following sections describe each of the seven stages in the escalation cycle, including strategies teachers can use to mitigate escalation at each stage. "Summary and Checklist for Escalation Cycle" and "Intervention Plan for Escalation Cycle" (pages 118–120) provide templates teachers can use to monitor the escalation cycle and plan an intervention.

Calm

During the calm phase, the student stays on task and engaged in classroom activities. He or she participates, responds to directions and praise, and maintains appropriate interactions with classmates and teachers. During this stage, the teacher's goal is to maintain the student's current state of mind. To do so, ensure that instruction is aligned to the student's instructional level and implement proactive strategies to reinforce a calm demeanor (such as giving the student a quiet area in the room to use).

Trigger

During the trigger phase, the student experiences a trigger that evokes tension and emotional unrest in the student. A *trigger* is an action or event that begins the escalation cycle. It can be a single event (such as a disagreement with a friend during lunch) or a gradual buildup of events (such as a lack of sleep each night). Triggers usually arise when a student is denied something he or she wants, has an unresolved conflict, or experiences something negative. Triggers can occur at school (such as peer conflicts, poor grades, or correction procedures) or at home (such as health problems, substance abuse, or family conflicts).

Teachers can have trouble managing triggers that occur outside of school hours. Generally speaking, teachers can offset triggers using two methods: (1) formal problem solving and (2) teaching behaviors. Formal problem solving involves changes within the classroom and assistance from others, such as curriculum changes or identifying certain levels of support the student needs. Teaching behaviors involves teaching missing behavioral skills in order to help the student manage triggers on his or her own.

Agitation

An unresolved trigger can lead to the agitation phase, during which the student's overall behavior becomes unfocused and off task. This stage can last for a considerable period of time as tension gradually builds. During this stage, the student may become noticeably agitated or nonresponsive. A teacher might see physical indicators (such as staring into space, darting eyes, busy hands, or comments that do not align with the conversation at hand). The student may also withdraw from others, become less talkative, and stop responding to feedback or direction.

During the agitation phase, typical teacher responses to misbehavior (such as repeating a request) can inadvertently escalate the student's misbehavior. To successfully navigate this stage, therefore, the teacher must know the student very well. Generally speaking, the goal is to calm the student down so that she can regain focus. The earlier the teacher intervenes, the stronger the chances of de-escalation. Provide the student with space, offer assurances, and allow time for activities such as taking a break, reading a book, or drawing.

While it may seem counterproductive to allow the student to work on a preferred activity during this phase, remember that, during this phase, the goal is not to ensure that the student completes the instructional activity. The goal is to avoid escalation. As the student builds self-management skills, the teacher can begin imposing normal expectations. Over time, the student learns to use his or her strategies when triggered and then makes up the missed work or activity. Keeping track of the length of agitation is also helpful. While it may be frustrating that the student still becomes agitated at times, if the length of the agitation phase decreases as the student's coping skills increase, then the student is becoming more successful. The initial goal might be to reduce the duration or frequency of the behavior, rather than to immediately aim for zero occurrences of the behavior.

Acceleration

When a student enters the acceleration phase, the teacher will notice a rapid and marked increase in behavior. The student engages in behavior to elicit reactions from others. For example, the student may argue, question assignments, make inappropriate comments, whine, cry, destroy property, or make threats. The student might also follow directions, but be intentionally disruptive at the same time. For example, the student may comply with a request to move his chair to a designated area, but choose to drag the chair on the ground in order to make a loud, disruptive noise. He may scribble his name poorly on a paper when asked to write his name. Here, the student is superficially compliant, but is not compliant with the expected criterion (in this case, "Move your chair quietly" or "Write your name neatly").

As the student actively seeks a reaction from others, the teacher must keep two considerations in mind. First, remain calm, direct, and brief when interacting with the student. Speak respectfully and privately to the student, as creating a scene can further escalate the situation. Try providing choice (for example, "You can complete your work here in class or you can earn detention"). Second, avoid negative interactions by disengaging with the student if he or she begins to argue. Use precision commands and walk away.

Generally, teachers can follow a particular procedure when confronting a student in the acceleration phase. Before a problem ever occurs, first ensure that all students have reviewed a list of possible consequences and enacted the classroom expectations in role-play scenarios. When a student does enter the acceleration phase, always present information as a choice within the student's control. Frame the two behaviors—meeting expectations versus causing a problem—as two options with different consequences. Table 7.4 provides two examples of responses to an accelerating student, with one framed as a choice and one framed as a demand.

Table 7.4: Positive and Negative Responses to a Student in the Acceleration Phase

Response	Sentence Frame	Example
Framed as a Choice	When I see [undesired behavior], it tells me you are choosing [result]. If you want to [desired result], then you should [desired behavior].	When I see you walking around and not sitting at your desk, it tells me you are choosing to do your work during lunch recess. If you want to go to lunch recess, then you will choose to sit down and finish your work.
Framed as a Demand	You need to stop [undesired behavior] or [result].	You need to sit down or you won't get lunch recess.

After giving the student a choice, give him or her some time to make a decision (one minute or less). During this wait time, walk away and attend to other students. Next, follow through. Observe the student to determine what choice he or she has made. The student may have decided to adhere to expectations; however, do not allow the student to partially comply (for example, by completing work carelessly or with minimal effort). In order to avoid an undesirable consequence, the student must choose to fully meet expectations. Finally, debrief with the student to process his or her behavior once the student is compliant with directions. Usually, this debrief can take place after the student has worked on the intended task for a while or before starting a new activity. Ask reflective questions such as the following.

1. What happened?

2. What was your behavior?

3. What was your concern or need?

4. What could you do differently next time that would be acceptable?

5. What are you expected to do next?

Only conduct this debrief if the student has chosen to comply. If the student's behavior escalates to the next phase, do not attempt to debrief.

Peak

In the peak phase, the student has escalated to aggressive, destructive, or out-of-control behavior. In this stage, the student poses a serious threat to the safety of herself and others. This phase may include destruction of property, assault, self-abuse, and tantrums. When a student reaches the peak phase, the teacher must primarily focus on student safety. Isolate the student from others and allow the escalation to run its course. Eventually, the student will calm down, but until then, staff should avoid interacting with her. Instead, focus on ensuring the safety of all students, including the escalating student. In the short term, follow the school's safety procedures. In the long term, consider a formal intervention plan that includes counseling and other forms of mental or emotional support.

De-Escalation

The student slowly returns to a moderate emotional state during the de-escalation phase, which occurs during isolation. The student may appear unfocused or confused and behave in a fairly subdued manner. A student in the de-escalation phase has had time to decompress, regain focus, and start privately working on an independent assignment.

Once the student becomes responsive and calm, meet briefly with him or her and, if applicable, with school leaders and counseling staff. Identify the consequences and any restorative steps the student should take before re-entering the classroom (such as fixing destroyed property, apologizing, accepting consequences, and so on). Develop a gradual plan for re-entry. Sometimes the student gradually earns her way back into a class or activity. Keep in mind that discussing consequences can lead to agitation and escalation. If this happens, disengage immediately. Ensure that the student is ready to discuss the situation by simply asking the student or by observing the student's behavior. If school officials send the student home, schedule the debriefing session for a later date. Once the student understands the consequences and makes restorative amends, she returns to normal class activities.

Recovery

Although the student may feel agitated and subdued during the recovery phase, she behaves in a relatively cooperative and calm manner. At this time, the student has returned to class but may prefer to work independently and demonstrate a lack of eagerness to participate in group work or class discussion. If necessary, the teacher can conduct a more in-depth debriefing session that focuses on problem solving. Allow the student to ease back into the normal schedule for a period of time before initiating the problem-solving debriefing.

Whereas debriefing in the de-escalation phase relates specifically to the immediate effects of the student's outburst, the problem-solving debriefing in the recovery phase focuses on long-term action steps. First, explain the purpose of the conversation—to focus on problem solving and developing a plan to avoid another outburst. Work through a set of four questions that help the student identify replacement behaviors to use in the future:

1. What was the behavior that was unacceptable?

2. What do you think led you to use that behavior?

3. What can you do differently next time?

4. What would help you use that new behavior?

Provide opportunities for the student to practice these replacement behaviors and revisit the plan within the next several days to ensure its helpfulness and appropriateness. After the meeting, focus on the normal routine and explicitly look for appropriate behavior from the student. Encourage participation and reinforce the replacement behavior.

Summary

Even with a well-developed classroom management system, some students will still require individualized attention to display appropriate behavior. Using precision commands, offering choices for tasks, and building behavioral momentum are a few strategies to use with students who continue to misbehave. A few students may have more serious outbursts, but these typically follow a predictable escalation cycle, which requires the teacher to use different strategies at different stages to intervene.

Chapter 7: Comprehension Questions

1. What does using behavioral momentum entail?

2. What is the difference between an antecedent strategy and a consequence strategy?

3. Why is it necessary to teach a replacement behavior?

4. What are the stages of the escalation cycle?

Antecedent and Consequence Tracking Form

To use this form, record each instance of the behavior with the date and time that it occurred, and then place check marks next to all of the antecedents (listed in the Antecedents column) and the consequences (listed in the Consequences column). You will need one copy of this form for each instance of the behavior.

Note: This is just an example of a tracking form. You may wish to alter the options for the antecedents and consequences based on your classroom.

Behavior to track (define the behavior in observable and measurable terms): _____				
Date / Time	**Antecedents (Mark what happened before the behavior)**			**Consequences (Mark what happened after the behavior)**
	Activity or Setting	**Tasks**	**With Whom**	**Get/Obtain Responses**

	Activity or Setting	**Tasks**	**With Whom**	**Get/Obtain Responses**	**Avoid/Escape Responses**
	☐ Reading ☐ Writing ☐ Math ☐ Science ☐ Social studies ☐ Transition ☐ Lunchtime ☐ Recess ☐ Study hall ☐ Library ☐ Computer ☐ Other:	☐ Work demand or request ☐ Verbal direction or request ☐ Removal of item ☐ Writing task ☐ Reading task ☐ Spelling task ☐ Noisy room ☐ Errors or correction with work ☐ Change from routine ☐ Other:	☐ Alone (no attention) ☐ Whole-class instruction ☐ Small group ☐ Independent work ☐ Other:	☐ Teacher talked with student ☐ Peer(s) interacted with student ☐ Worked on another activity or a preferred activity ☐ Obtained an item (for example, preferred book) ☐ Obtained a task (for example, computer time) ☐ Other:	☐ Did not complete work or avoided work ☐ Spent time in hallway or area alone (removed attention) ☐ Moved into a different area or setting ☐ Other:

Behavior Assessment Interview

1. What is the behavior of concern? Please describe the behavior in concrete, observable, and measurable terms.

2. How often does the behavior occur daily? Circle one.

   A. <1   D. 7–9

   B. 1–3   E. 10–12

   C. 4–6   F. >12

Antecedents

Think of the things that occur before the behavior and respond to the following questions. If the answer to a question is yes, further describe the behavior or situation.

1. Does the behavior occur during a certain type of task?

2. Does the behavior occur more often during easy tasks?

3. Does the behavior occur more often during difficult tasks?

4. Does the behavior occur more often during certain subjects?

5. Does the behavior occur more often during new subject material?

6. Does the behavior occur more often when a request is made to stop an activity?

7. Does the behavior occur more often when a request is made to start an activity?

page 1 of 3

8. Does the behavior occur more often during transition times?

9. Does the behavior occur more often when a request has been denied?

10. Does the behavior occur more often when a specific person is in the room?

11. Does the behavior occur more often when a specific person is absent from the room?

12. Are there other behaviors that precede the behavior?

13. Are there events at home that seem to precede the behavior?

14. Does the behavior occur more in certain settings? Circle all that apply.

   A. Large group
   B. Small group
   C. Independent work
   D. One-on-one interaction

   E. Common areas
   F. Lunch/cafeteria
   G. Other: _____

Consequences

Think of the things that occur after the behavior and respond to the following questions. If the answer to a question is yes, further describe the behavior or situation.

1. Does the student receive access to a preferred activity?

2. Does the student receive access to a preferred object?

3. Does the task the student was given stop?

page 2 of 3

4. Is the student's behavior ignored?

5. Is the student removed from the setting (that is, given time alone)?

6. Does the student receive attention from classmates or peers?

7. Does the student receive teacher attention in the form of

    A. praise?

    B. redirection?

    C. interrupting the teacher?

    D. a reprimand?

8. Is there any task that you stopped presenting to the student as a result of the behavior?

9. Does the student receive any sort of positive benefits or attention from the behavior?

Source: Adapted from Steege, M. W., & Watson, T. S. (2009). *Conducting school-based functional behavioral assessments: A practitioner's guide* (2nd ed.). New York: Guilford Press.

Intervention Design Template

Use this form to design an intervention for an individual behavior. In the first table, describe the antecedent, the behavior itself, and the consequence. In the second table, write a detailed plan for how you will prevent the problem behavior and punish or put it on extinction, teach and reinforce the replacement behavior, and monitor the fidelity and effectiveness of your plan.

Problem Behavior

Antecedent	Behavior	Consequence

Intervention

Point of Intervention	Component	Plan for Intervention
Antecedent	Prevention	
Behavior	Teaching	
Consequence	Reinforcement	
	Extinction and Punishment	
Evaluation	Evaluation of Fidelity	
	Evaluation of Effectiveness	

Source: Adapted from Newton, J. S., Horner, R. H., Todd, A. T., Algozzine, R. F., & Algozzine, K. M. (2012). A pilot study of a problem-solving model for team decision making. *Education and Treatment of Children, 35*(1), 25–49.

Summary and Checklist for Escalation Cycle

Student Name: _____   Date: _____

For each phase, check all that apply.

Phase 1: Calm

Student behaves cooperatively and acceptably

- ☐ Staying on task during instruction and work
- ☐ Adherence to rules and expectations
- ☐ Responsiveness to praise
- ☐ Appropriate behavior
- ☐ Goal-oriented behavior
- ☐ Other: _____

Phase 2: Trigger

Student encounters one or more unresolved problems

At School	**Outside of School**
☐ Conflicts (peer or teacher)	☐ High-needs home
☐ Denial of a need	☐ Health issues
☐ Negative incident	☐ Nutrition needs
☐ Change in routines	☐ Inadequate sleep
☐ Peer provocations	☐ Diagnosed emotional or behavioral disorder
☐ Pressure from the demands of school	☐ Substance abuse
☐ Ineffective problem solving	☐ Gangs and deviant peer groups
☐ Facing errors in instruction	☐ Other: _____
☐ Other: _____	

Phase 3: Agitation

Student behaves distractedly

Increases in Behavior	**Decreases in Behavior**
☐ Darting eyes	☐ Staring into space
☐ Busy hands	☐ Avoiding eye contact
☐ Moving in and out of groups	☐ Nonconversational language
☐ Alternating between off-task and on-task behavior	☐ Contained hands (for example, hands in pockets, arms crossed)
☐ Other: _____	☐ Withdrawal from groups
	☐ Other: _____

page 1 of 2

Phase 4: Acceleration

Student tries to engage staff and peers to garner attention or incite a response

- ☐ Questioning and arguing
- ☐ Noncompliance and defiance
- ☐ Off-task behavior
- ☐ Provocation of others
- ☐ Criterion problems (for example, completing work poorly on purpose, following directions in a passive-aggressive manner, or disruptively following directions)
- ☐ Breaking rules
- ☐ Whining or crying
- ☐ Avoidance and escape
- ☐ Threats and intimidation toward others
- ☐ Verbal abuse
- ☐ Other: _____

Phase 5: Peak

Student behaves in an out-of-control, aggressive, or destructive manner

- ☐ Destruction of property
- ☐ Physical attacks
- ☐ Self-abuse
- ☐ Severe tantrums
- ☐ Running away
- ☐ Other: _____

Phase 6: De-Escalation

Student behaves in a confused and unfocused manner

- ☐ Confusion
- ☐ Reconciliation
- ☐ Withdrawal
- ☐ Denial
- ☐ Blaming others
- ☐ Responsiveness to directions
- ☐ Responsiveness to hands-on or mechanical tasks
- ☐ Avoidance of discussion
- ☐ Avoidance of debriefing
- ☐ Other: _____

Phase 7: Recovery

Student is no longer agitated but is reluctant to interact with others

- ☐ Preference for independent work or activity, often busywork
- ☐ Subdued behavior in group work or class discussions
- ☐ Defensive behavior
- ☐ Other: _____

Source: Adapted from Colvin, G. (2004). *Managing the cycle of acting-out behavior in the classroom.* Eugene, OR: Behavior Associates.

page 2 of 2

Intervention Plan for Escalation Cycle

Student Name: _____   Date: _____

Write down the behavior(s) the student performs at each phase, as well as potential teacher response strategies.

Escalation Phase	Student Behaviors	Teacher Response Strategies
Calm		
Trigger		
Agitation		
Acceleration		
Peak		
De-Escalation		
Recovery		

EPILOGUE

Historical efforts to manage behavior in schools and classrooms have been largely ineffective or have come with unintended costs. For example, the use of suspension and expulsion fails to decrease misbehavior and places students who are suspended or expelled at a higher risk for dropping out and being incarcerated later in life. Furthermore, administrators use suspension and expulsion inequitably, with nonwhite students vastly overrepresented. Additionally, the use of punishment-only approaches is associated with continued misbehavior, escalating behavior, and continued punishment.

The premise of this book is that a more proactive and instructional approach to managing student behavior is much more effective than what is traditionally seen in schools. Just as academics are actively taught to students, behavior can and should be taught in the same manner. Instead of assuming that all misbehavior is a result of willful disobedience and punishing students accordingly, teachers can take an instructional view and treat misbehavior as an opportunity to teach a more appropriate alternative. First, teachers can reduce the likelihood of problem behavior by directly teaching expectations and rules, establishing structure and procedures in the classroom, and ensuring active engagement during instruction. With this base established, teachers can reinforce desired behaviors and use a range of strategies to correct problem behaviors when they do arise.

Teachers can benefit from practical, solid guidelines on implementing strategies that reduce unwanted behavior. While this book focused on the classroom level, the principles presented here are also applicable to schoolwide behavior models. Teachers can use this book to develop classroom management plans, but these concepts can also be a stepping stone toward a schoolwide climate and discipline model. On the whole, a positive, instruction-based approach to behavior management is the most effective means of creating a friendly, stable classroom where learning time is maximized.

APPENDIX

ANSWERS TO COMPREHENSION QUESTIONS

Answers to Chapter 2: Comprehension Questions

1. *What are the similarities and differences between expectations and rules?*

   Expectations and rules both describe behavior that is expected in the classroom. They are also positively stated, brief, and limited in number. They differ in that expectations are broader and apply to all settings and events, whereas rules are specific and apply to a limited number of settings and events.

2. *Describe two methods for identifying expectations. What are the pros and cons of each?*

   Two methods for identifying expectations are: (1) the teacher creates expectations before the start of the school year based on the school's mission and vision, or (2) the teacher holds a discussion with students to collaboratively create a set of expectations. The first option allows the teacher to introduce expectations to students at the very beginning of the year but does not involve students in the process. The second option includes students and may therefore produce more buy-in from students but delays the teaching of expectations somewhat.

3. *Why would a teacher want to provide a rationale for an expectation when teaching it to students?*

   Providing a rationale creates a broader understanding of the expectation beyond simply following rules because they are rules. The rationale can serve as a justification for following the expectation and can be used to transition from providing tangible, external reinforcement to providing intrinsic, natural reinforcement.

4. *What are some ways the expectations can be reviewed throughout the school year?*

   The expectations can be reviewed in various ways. Students can read novels and stories about the expectations or be asked to reflect on how characters showed (or didn't show) an expectation. Students can write essays about how characters exhibited expectations, or they can develop songs, videos, and skits on the expectations as part of a fine arts class (such as music, art, film, or graphic design classes). The use of posters and other visual methods can provide students with continuous reminders of the expectations. Weekly or monthly focus lessons can make the expectations more explicit and deepen students' understanding. Teachers can conduct booster sessions if it becomes apparent that students have forgotten one or more expectations.

Answers to Chapter 3: Comprehension Questions

1. *Why do students need to be taught procedures?*

   Students benefit from procedures because they provide a clear script for how to complete tasks and achieve goals. They also allow students to operate independently and perform tasks quickly in ways that do not distract others or take time away from instruction.

2. *How can the physical layout of a classroom decrease problem behavior?*

   Certain physical layouts can provoke problem behavior, so changing the environment can help prevent such issues. For example, high-traffic areas can be organized so that students do not bump into each other or crowd around one area. Creating a classroom environment that minimizes distraction and interruption is an important first step in effective classroom management.

3. *Why are transitions particularly important?*

   Transitions, by nature, create opportunity for distraction and unwanted behavior. The longer they take to complete, the greater the likelihood that students will become disruptive and off task. Creating and teaching transition procedures keeps students focused and transitions brief.

4. *What is the general format for teaching procedures?*

   Teaching procedures follows a model, lead, test format. Teachers directly teach the procedure and model it for students. Students are given time to practice the procedure and then are tested to ensure they have learned it.

Answers to Chapter 4: Comprehension Questions

1. *What are examples of each type of reinforcement?*

   Short-term rewards can be tickets, tokens, stamps, or signatures that students receive frequently when they display appropriate behavior. Long-term rewards are larger rewards, such as access to a school store or extra privileges. Students often save up their short-term rewards to "purchase" a long-term reward. Intermittent rewards are given at random times based on predetermined criteria and can be tangible objects (such as trophies) or intangible rewards (like getting to be first in line).

2. *What are the critical elements of behavior-specific praise?*

   Behavior-specific praise should both accurately describe the behavior and provide approval of it.

3. *What are some things to consider when designing rewards?*

   Short-term rewards should be small, portable, and easy to track. Other considerations include giving rewards out often and frequently, especially early on, so that students buy into them. Short-term rewards should be distributed equitably and paired with praise so students know why they received a reward. Consider surveying students' preferences and designing short- and long-term rewards that capture their interest.

4. *Describe the three types of group contingency.*

   The three types of group contingency are (1) interdependent, (2) dependent, and (3) independent. Interdependent means that the entire class must reach the criterion for everyone to earn the reward. Dependent means that the whole class receives a reward based on the success of one student or a small group of students. Independent means that each student in the class earns the reward separately, based on his or her own behavior.

Answers to Chapter 5: Comprehension Questions

1. *What are some benefits of active engagement?*

   Active engagement is associated with increased time on task and more accurate responses (that is, improved academic achievement). Teachers also benefit from active engagement because students' responses provide information about their learning progress.

2. *What are the general types of student responses?*

   Opportunities to respond are categorized as verbal, written, and action. Verbal responses are ones in which students provide spoken answers. Written responses require students to write down their answers. Action responses include the use of gestures, technology tools, or premade signs (such as response cards).

3. *What is the difference between individual and choral responses?*

   Calling on one student to provide a response is individual response. Individual responses can be used when answers are short or longer. Choral responses involve all students responding simultaneously. They are most helpful when responses are short and when there is only one correct answer. Research suggests a balance of 30 percent individual responses and 70 percent choral responses in a given instructional session.

4. *What are the desired rates of OTRs for different types of instruction?*

   Students should have a rate of four to six OTRs per minute for new material and eight to twelve for previously learned material. For whole-class instruction, researchers recommend between three and six OTRs per minute versus eight to twelve for small-group instruction.

Answers to Chapter 6: Comprehension Questions

1. *What is the difference between reinforcement and punishment?*

   Reinforcement increases the rate of a behavior, whereas punishment decreases the rate of a behavior.

2. *What do the terms* negative *and* positive *mean in the context of behavior management? What do negative and positive reinforcement and punishment look like in practice?*

   Negative means removing something; *positive* means adding or applying something. Negative reinforcement involves taking away something undesirable. Positive reinforcement involves giving a student a desirable reward. Negative punishment is the removal of something desirable whereas positive punishment is the application of something undesirable or aversive.

3. *How can reinforcement be used to decrease problem behavior?*

   When the use of a more appropriate replacement behavior is strengthened through reinforcement, the student is likely to stop using the problem behavior. Reinforcing appropriate behavior leads a student to use that behavior more frequently, while discouraging unwanted behavior because it is not being reinforced.

4. *Explain the reasoning behind the order of the management hierarchy.*

   The hierarchy uses positive, nonaversive methods—that is, reinforcement—first. Many problem behaviors can be managed by reinforcing more appropriate behaviors, which removes the need for teachers to actively punish a problem behavior. If the unwanted behavior persists, negative punishment should be used next. It sends a stronger message to the student that his or her behavior is unacceptable but focuses on a loss of privileges rather than more aversive applications. If behavioral data warrant its use, a teacher can move to the final level—positive punishment. The application of unpleasant stimuli, such as overcorrection, should only be used if absolutely necessary. The order of the management hierarchy ensures that behaviors are managed in accordance with their severity.

Answers to Chapter 7: Comprehension Questions

1. *What does using behavioral momentum entail?*

   Behavioral momentum involves presenting a student with high-probability requests prior to presenting the student with a low-probability request. That is, the teacher asks the student to complete a few small steps or easy tasks to give the student confidence and get him or her moving in the right direction before asking the student to complete a larger or less desirable task.

2. *What is the difference between an antecedent strategy and a consequence strategy?*

   Antecedent strategies focus on prevention or reducing the chances of the behavior occurring in the first place. Consequence strategies focus on the consequences of the behavior (that is, reinforcement or punishment) and involve manipulating the events after the behavior to change the likelihood that it will occur again.

3. *Why is it necessary to teach a replacement behavior?*

   Behavior serves a purpose. When students are expected to stop using one behavior, they will need a replacement behavior that serves the same purpose. If they do not have a replacement, students will resort to using the old behavior. By giving students more appropriate behaviors to use, teachers can make the problem behavior irrelevant.

4. *What are the stages of the escalation cycle?*

   There are seven stages of the escalation cycle: (1) calm, (2) trigger, (3) agitation, (4) acceleration, (5) peak, (6) de-escalation, and (7) recovery.

REFERENCES AND RESOURCES

Akin-Little, K. A., Eckert, T. L., Lovett, B. J., & Little, S. G. (2004). Extrinsic reinforcement in the classroom: Bribery or best practice. *School Psychology Review, 33*(3), 344–362.

Alberto, P. A., & Troutman, A. C. (2013). *Applied behavior analysis for teachers* (9th ed.). New York: Pearson.

Alter, P., Walker, J., & Landers, E. (2013). Teachers' perceptions of students' challenging behavior and the impact of teacher demographics. *Education and Treatment of Children, 36*(4), 51–69.

American Civil Liberties Union. (n.d.). *What is the school-to-prison pipeline?* Accessed at www.aclu.org /racial-justice/what-school-prison-pipeline on December 2, 2014.

American Psychological Association Zero Tolerance Task Force. (2008). Are zero tolerance policies effective in the schools?: An evidentiary review and recommendations. *American Psychologist, 63*(9), 852–862.

Anhalt, K., McNeil, C. B., & Bahl, A. B. (1998). The ADHD classroom kit: A whole-classroom approach for managing disruptive behavior. *Psychology in the Schools, 35*(1), 67–79.

Archer, A., & Hughes, C. (2010, June/November). *Teaching explicitly: Evidence-based instruction for students with learning difficulties.* Sponsored by the Utah Department of Education, Salt Lake City, UT.

Baer, D. M., Wolf, M. M., & Risley, T. R. (1968). Some current dimensions of applied behavior analysis. *Journal of Applied Behavior Analysis, 1*(1), 91–97.

Balcazar, F., Hopkins, B. L., & Suarez, Y. (1986). A critical, objective review of performance feedback. *Journal of Organizational Behavior Management, 7*(3/4), 65–89.

Bambara, L. M., & Kern, L. (Eds.). (2005). *Individualized supports for students with problem behaviors: Designing positive behavior plans.* New York: Guilford Press.

Bettenhausen, S. (1998). Make proactive modifications to your classroom. *Intervention in School and Clinic, 33*(3), 182–183.

Bohanon, H., Fenning, P., Carney, K., Minnis, M., Anderson-Harriss, S., Moroz, K., et al. (2006). Schoolwide application of positive behavior support in an urban high school: A case study. *Journal of Positive Behavior Interventions, 8*(3), 131–145.

Bowditch, C. (1993). Getting rid of troublemakers: High school disciplinary procedures and the production of dropouts. *Social Problems, 40*(4), 493–507.

Bowen, J., Jenson, W. R., & Clark, E. (2004). *School-based interventions for students with behavior problems.* New York: Springer.

Bradshaw, C. P., Koth, C. W., Bevans, K. B., Ialongo, N., & Leaf, P. J. (2008). The impact of school-wide positive behavioral interventions and supports (PBIS) on the organizational health of elementary schools. *School Psychology Quarterly, 23*(4), 462–473.

Bradshaw, C. P., Mitchell, M. M., & Leaf, P. J. (2010). Examining the effects of Schoolwide Positive Behavioral Interventions and Supports on student outcomes: Results from a randomized controlled effectiveness trial in elementary schools. *Journal of Positive Behavior Interventions, 12*(3), 133–148.

Brophy, J. E. (1981). Teacher praise: A functional analysis. *Review of Educational Research, 51,* 5–32.

Brophy, J., & Good, T. (1986). Teacher behavior and student achievement. In M. Wittrock (Ed.), *Handbook of research on teaching* (3rd ed., pp. 328–375). New York: Macmillan.

Buck, G. (1999). Smoothing the rough edges of classroom transitions. *Intervention in School and Clinic, 34*(4), 224–235.

Buluc, B. (2006). An analysis of classroom rules in secondary schools in Turkey. *Educational Research Quarterly, 29*(3), 30–51.

Burnett, P. C. (2001). Elementary students' preferences for teacher praise. *Journal of Classroom Interaction, 36*(1), 16–23.

Cameron, J., Banko, K. M., & Pierce, W. D. (2001). Pervasive negative effects of rewards on intrinsic motivation: The myth continues. *Behavior Analyst, 24*(1), 1–44.

Cameron, J., & Pierce, W. D. (1994). Reinforcement, reward, and intrinsic motivation: A meta-analysis. *Review of Educational Research, 64*(3), 363–423.

Campbell, S., & Skinner, C. H. (2004). Combining explicit timing with an interdependent group contingency program to decrease transition times: An investigation of the Timely Transitions Game. *Journal of Applied School Psychology, 20*(2), 11–27.

Canter, L. (2010). *Assertive discipline: Positive behavior management for today's classroom* (4th ed.). Bloomington, IN: Solution Tree Press.

Carnine, D. W. (1976). Effects of two teacher-presentation rates on off-task behavior, answering correctly, and participation. *Journal of Applied Behavior Analysis, 9*(2), 199–206.

Carr, E. G., Dunlap, G., Horner, R. H., Koegel, R. L., Turnbull, A. P., Sailor, W., et al. (2002). Positive behavior support: Evolution of an applied science. *Journal of Positive Behavior Interventions, 4*(1), 4–20.

Cavanaugh, B. (2013). Performance feedback and teachers' use of praise and opportunities to respond: A review of the literature. *Education and Treatment of Children, 36*(1), 111–137.

Centers for Disease Control and Prevention. (2012). *Youth violence: Facts at a glance.* Accessed at www.cdc.gov/violenceprevention/pdf/yv-datasheet-a.pdf on December 2, 2014.

Chalk, K., & Bizo, L. A. (2004). Specific praise improves on-task behaviour and numeracy enjoyment: A study of year 4 pupils engaged in the numeracy hour. *Educational Psychology in Practice, 20*(4), 335–352.

Civil Rights Project, & Advancement Project. (2000, June 15). *Opportunities suspended: The devastating consequences of zero tolerance and school discipline policies.* Accessed at http://civilrightsproject.ucla .edu/research/k-12-education/school-discipline/opportunities-suspended-the-devastating -consequences-of-zero-tolerance-and-school-discipline-policies/crp-opportunities-suspended-zero -tolerance-2000.pdf on December 2, 2014.

Coalition for Juvenile Justice (2001). *Abandoned in the back row: New lessons in education and delinquency prevention—2001 annual report.* Accessed at www.juvjustice.org/media/resources/resource _122.pdf on December 3, 2014.

Cohen, J. (1988). *Statistical power analysis for the behavioral sciences* (2nd ed.). Hillsdale, NJ: Erlbaum.

Colvin, G. (2004). *Managing the cycle of acting-out behavior in the classroom.* Eugene, OR: Behavior Associates.

Colvin, G. (2007). *7 steps for developing a proactive schoolwide discipline plan: A guide for principals and leadership teams.* Thousand Oaks, CA: Corwin Press.

Colvin, G., Sugai, G., & Patching, W. (1993). Precorrection: An instructional approach for managing predictable problem behaviors. *Intervention in School and Clinic, 28*(3), 143–150.

Costenbader, V., & Markson, S. (1998). School suspension: A study with secondary school students. *Journal of School Psychology, 36*(1), 59–82.

Council for Exceptional Children. (1987). *Academy for effective instruction: Working with mildly handicapped students.* Reston, VA: Author.

Crone, D. A., & Horner, R. H. (2003). *Building positive behavior support systems in schools: Functional behavioral assessment.* New York: Guilford Press.

Daly, E. J., III, Lentz, F. E., Jr., & Boyer, J. (1996). The instructional hierarchy: A conceptual model for understanding the effective components of reading interventions. *School Psychology Quarterly, 11*(4), 369–386.

Daly, E. J., III, & Martens, B. K. (1994). A comparison of three interventions for increasing oral reading performance: Application of the instructional hierarchy. *Journal of Applied Behavior Analysis, 27*(3), 459–469.

Darch, C. B., & Kame'enui, E. J. (2003). *Instructional classroom management: A proactive approach to behavior management* (2nd ed.). New York: Merrill.

Darch, C. B., Miller, A., & Shippen, P. (1998). Instructional classroom management: A proactive model for teaching and managing student behavior. *Beyond Behavior, 9*(3), 1–2.

Deci, E. L. (1971). Effects of externally mediated rewards on intrinsic motivation. *Journal of Personality and Social Psychology, 18*(1), 105–115.

Deci, E. L., Koestner, R., & Ryan, R. M. (2001). Extrinsic rewards and intrinsic motivation in education: Reconsidered once again. *Review of Educational Research, 71*(1), 1–27.

Deitz, S. M., & Repp, A. C. (1973). Decreasing classroom misbehavior through the use of DRL schedules of reinforcement. *Journal of Applied Behavior Analysis, 6*(3), 457–463.

Deitz, S. M., & Repp, A. C. (1983). Reducing behavior through reinforcement. *Exceptional Education Quarterly, 3*(4), 34–46.

DePry, R. L., & Sugai, G. (2002). The effect of active supervision and pre-correction on minor behavioral incidents in a sixth grade general education classroom. *Journal of Behavioral Education, 11*(4), 255–267.

Dunlap, G., Harrower, J., & Fox, L. (2005). Understanding the environmental determinants of problem behaviors. In L. M. Bambara & L. Kern (Eds.), *Individualized supports for students with behavior problems: Designing positive behavior plans* (pp. 25–46). New York: Guilford.

Dunson, R. M., Hughes, J. N., & Jackson, T. W. (1994). Effect of behavioral consultation on student and teacher behavior. *Journal of School Psychology, 32*(3), 247–266.

Dweck, C. (2008). *Mindset: The new psychology of success.* New York: Ballantine Books.

Ekstrom, R. B., Goertz, M. E., Pollack, J. M., & Rock, D. A. (1986). Who drops out of high school and why?: Findings from a national study. *Teachers College Record, 87*(3), 357–373. Accessed at www.tcrecord.org/Content.asp?ContentId=688 on December 2, 2014.

Ennis, R. P., Schwab, J., & Jolivette, K. (2012). Using precorrection as a secondary-tier intervention for reducing problem behaviors in instructional and noninstructional settings. *Beyond Behavior, 22*(1), 40–47.

Epstein, M., Atkins, M., Cullinan, D., Kutash, K., & Weaver, R. (2008, September). *Reducing behavior problems in the elementary school classroom: A practice guide* (NCEE #2008–012). Washington, DC: National Center for Education Evaluation and Regional Assistance, Institute of Education Sciences, U.S. Department of Education.

Evans, K. R., & Lester, J. N. (2012). Zero tolerance: Moving the conversation forward. *Intervention in School and Clinic, 48*(2), 108–114.

Evertson, C. M., & Emmer, E. T. (2013). *Classroom management for elementary teachers* (9th ed.). Boston: Pearson.

Fay, J., & Funk, D. (1995). *Teaching with love and logic: Taking control of the classroom.* Golden, CO: Love and Logic Press.

Feldman, S. (2003). The place for praise. *Teaching PreK–8, 33*, 6.

Filcheck, H. A., McNeil, C. B., Greco, L. A., & Bernard, R. S. (2004). Using a whole-class token economy and coaching of teacher skills in a preschool classroom to manage disruptive behavior. *Psychology in the Schools, 41*(3), 351–361.

Fisher, D., & Frey, N. (Eds.). (2004). *Improving adolescent literacy: Strategies at work.* Upper Saddle River, NJ: Pearson.

Fisher, D., & Frey, N. (2008). *Better learning through structured teaching: A framework for the gradual release of responsibility.* Alexandria, VA: Association for Supervision and Curriculum Development.

Flora, S. R. (2000). Praise's magic reinforcement ratio: Five to one gets the job done. *The Behavior Analyst Today, 1,* 64–69.

Florida's Positive Behavior Support Project. (n.d.). Accessed at http://flpbs.fmhi.usf.edu/index.cfm on December 2, 2014.

Forehand, R. L., & McMahon, R. J. (1981). *Helping the noncompliant child: A clinician's guide to parent training.* New York: Guilford Press.

Foxx, R. M., & Bechtel, D. R. (1982). Overcorrection. In M. Hersen, R. Eisler, & P. Miller (Eds.), *Progress in behavior modification* (Vol. 13, pp. 227–288). New York: Academic Press.

Gable, R. A., Hester, P. H., Rock, M. L., & Hughes, K. G. (2009). Back to basics: Rules, praise, ignoring, and reprimands revisited. *Intervention in School and Clinic, 44*(4), 195–205.

George, H. P., Kincaid, D., & Pollard-Sage, J. (2009). Primary-tier interventions and supports. In W. Sailor, G. Dunlap, G. Sugai, & R. Horner (Eds.), *Handbook of positive behavior support* (pp. 375–394). New York: Springer.

Gonzalez, L., Brown, M. S., & Slate, J. R. (2008). Teachers who left the teaching profession: A qualitative understanding. *The Qualitative Report, 13*(1), 1–11.

Gottman, J. M. (1994). *Why marriages succeed or fail: And how you can make yours last.* New York: Simon & Schuster.

Greenberg, J., Putman, H., & Walsh, K. (2014). *Training our future teachers: Classroom management.* Washington, DC: National Council on Teacher Quality. Accessed at www.nctq.org/dmsView/Future _Teachers_Classroom_Management_NCTQ_Report on December 2, 2014.

Greenwood, C. R. (1997). Classwide peer tutoring. *Behavioral and Social Issues, 7*(1), 52–57.

Greenwood, C. R., Maheady, L., & Delquadri, J. (2002). Class-wide peer tutoring. In M. R. Shinn, H. M. Walker, & G. Stoner (Eds.), *Interventions for achievement and behavior problems II: Preventative and remedial approaches* (pp. 611–649). Bethesda, MD: National Association for School Psychologists.

Gresham, F. M. (2002). Teaching social skills to high-risk children and youth: Preventive and remedial strategies. In M. R. Shinn, H. M. Walker, & G. Stoner (Eds.), *Interventions for academic and behavior problems II: Preventive and remedial approaches* (pp. 403–432). Bethesda, MD: National Association of School Psychologists.

Gresham, F. M. (2009). Evolution of the treatment integrity concept: Current status and future directions. *School Psychology Review, 38*(4), 533–540.

Gunter, P. L., Reffel, J., Barnett, C. A., Lee, J. L., & Patrick, J. (2004). Academic response rates in elementary-school classrooms. *Education and Treatment of Children, 27*(2), 105–113.

Harlacher, J. E., Walker, N. J. N., & Sanford, A. K. (2010). The "I" in RTI: Research-based factors for intensifying instruction. *Teaching Exceptional Children, 42*(6), 30–38.

Hattie, J. (2009). *Visible learning: A synthesis of over 800 meta-analyses relating to achievement.* New York: Routledge.

Hattie, J., & Timperley, H. (2007). The power of feedback. *Review of Educational Research, 77*(1), 81–112.

Haydon, T., Conroy, M. A., Scott, T. M., Sindelar, P. T., Barber, B. R., & Orlando, A. (2010). A comparison of three types of opportunities to respond on student academic and social behaviors. *Journal of Emotional and Behavioral Disorders, 18*(1), 27–40.

Haydon, T., Mancil, G. R., & Van Loan, C. (2009). Using opportunities to respond in a general education classroom: A case study. *Education and Treatment of Children, 32*(2), 267–278.

Haydon, T., Marsicano, R., & Scott, T. M. (2013). A comparison of choral and individual responding: A review of the literature. *Preventing School Failure, 57*(4), 181–188.

Herner, J. (1998, Winter). Discipline: To teach or to punish? *Counterpoint, National Association of State Directors of Special Education, 19*, 2.

Heward, W. L. (1994). Three "low-tech" strategies for increasing the frequency of active student response during group instruction. In R. Gardner, III, D. M. Sainato, J. O. Cooper, T. E. Heron, W. L. Heward, J. W. Eshleman, & T. A. Grossi (Eds.), *Behavior analysis in education: Focus on measurably superior instruction* (pp. 283–320). Pacific Grove, CA: Brooks/Cole.

Heward, W. L. (1997). Four validated instructional strategies. *Behavior and Social Issues, 7*(1), 43–51.

Hoffman, J. B., & DuPaul, C. J. (2000). Psychoeducational interventions for children and adolescents with attention-deficit/hyperactivity disorder. *Child and Adolescent Psychiatric Clinics of North America, 9*(3), 647–661.

Horner, R. H., Sugai, G., Smolkowski, K., Eber, L., Nakasato, J., Todd, A. W., et al. (2009). A randomized, wait-list controlled effectiveness trial assessing school-wide positive behavior support in elementary schools. *Journal of Positive Behavior Inverventions, 11*(3), 133–144.

Horner, R. H., Sugai, G., Todd, A. W., & Lewis-Palmer, T. (2005). School-wide positive behavior support: An alternative approach to discipline in schools. In L. M. Bambara & L. Kern (Eds.), *Individualized supports for students with problem behaviors: Designing positive behavior plans* (pp. 359–390). New York: Guilford.

Ingersoll, R. M. (2002, June). The teacher shortage: A case of wrong diagnosis and wrong prescription. *NASSP Bulletin, 86*(631), 16–31.

Ingersoll, R. M., & Smith, T. M. (2003). The wrong solution to the teacher shortage. *Educational Leadership, 60*(8), 30–33.

Institute of Education Sciences. (2007). *What works clearinghouse: ClassWide peer tutoring* (WWC Intervention report). Accessed at http://ies.ed.gov/ncee/wwc/pdf/intervention_reports/WWC_CWPT_070907.pdf on December 2, 2014.

Johnson, K. R., & Layng, T. V. J. (1994). The Morningside Model of generative instruction. In R. Gardner, III, D. M. Sainato, J. O. Cooper, T. E. Heron, W. L. Heward, J. Eshleman, & T. A. Grossi (Eds.), *Behavior analysis in education: Focus on measurably superior instruction* (pp. 173–197). Pacific Grove, CA: Brooks/Cole.

Kagan, S., & Kagan, M. (2009). *Kagan cooperative learning.* San Clemente, CA: Kagan.

Kame'enui, E. J. & Simmons, D. C. (1990). *Designing instructional strategies: The prevention of academic learning problems.* Columbus, OH: Merrill.

Kamps, D., Barbetta, P., Leonard, B., Delquadri, J., & Hall, R.V. (1994). Classwide peer tutoring: An integration strategy to improve reading skills and promote peer interaction among students with autism and general education peers. *Journal of Applied Behavior Analysis, 27*(1), 49–61.

Kern, L., White, G., & Gresham, F. M. (2007). Educating students with behavioral challenges. *Principal, 86,* 56–58.

Kerr, M. M., & Nelson, C. M. (2006). *Strategies for addressing behavior problems in the classroom* (5th ed.). Upper Saddle River, NJ: Pearson.

Kohn, A. (1993). *Punished by rewards: The trouble with gold stars, incentive plans, As, praise, and other bribes.* Boston: Houghton Mifflin.

Kratochwill, T. R., Elliott, S. N., & Callan-Stoiber, K. (2002). Best practices in school-based problem-solving consultation. In A. Thomas & J. Grimes (Eds.), *Best practices in school psychology IV* (pp. 583–608). Bethesda, MD: National Association of School Psychologists.

Kratochwill, T. R., & Shernoff, E. S. (2004). Evidence-based practice: Promoting evidence-based interventions in school psychology. *School Psychology Review, 33*(1), 34–48.

Lampi, A. R., Fenty, N. S., & Beaunae, C. (2005). Making the three Ps easier: Praise, proximity, and precorrection. *Beyond Behavior, 15*(1), 8–12.

Langland, S., Lewis-Palmer, T., & Sugai, G. (1998). Teaching respect in the classroom: An instructional approach. *Journal of Behavioral Education, 8,* 245–262.

Lewis, T. J., Colvin, G., & Sugai, G. (2000). The effects of pre-correction and active supervision on the recess behavior of elementary students. *Education and Treatment of Children, 23*(2), 109–121.

Lewis, T. J., Hudson, S., Richter, M., & Johnson, N. (2004). Scientifically supported practices in emotional and behavioral disorders: A proposed approach and brief review of current practices. *Behavioral Disorders, 29*(3), 247–259.

Lieberman, D. (n.d.). *The impact of school suspension, and a demand for passage of the Student Safety Act.* Accessed at www.nyclu.org/content/impact-of-school-suspensions-and-demand-passage-of-student-safety-act on December 2, 2014.

Little, E. (2005). Secondary school teachers' perceptions of student problem behaviours. *Educational Psychology, 25*(4), 369–377.

Losada, M., & Heaphy, E. (2004). The role of positivity and connectivity in the performance of business teams: A nonlinear dynamics model. *American Behavioral Scientist, 47*(6), 740–765.

Mace, F. C., Hock, M. L., Lalli, J. S., West, B. J., Belfiore, P., Pinter, E., et al. (1988). Behavioral momentum in the treatment of noncompliance. *Journal of Applied Behavioral Analysis, 21*(2), 123–141.

Mackay, S., McLaughlin, T. F., Weber, K., & Derby K. M. (2001). The use of precision requests to decrease noncompliance in the home and neighborhood: A case study. *Child and Family Behavior Therapy, 23*(3), 41–50.

MacSuga-Gage, A. S., Simonsen, B., & Briere, D. E. (2012). Effective teaching practices that promote a positive classroom environment. *Beyond Behavior, 22*(1), 14–22.

Marzano, R. J. (with Marzano, J. S., & Pickering, D. J.). (2003). *Classroom management that works: Research-based strategies for every teacher.* Alexandria, VA: Association for Supervision and Curriculum Development.

Marzano, R. J. (2007). *The art and science of teaching: A comprehensive framework for effective instruction.* Alexandria, VA: Association for Supervision and Curriculum Development.

Marzano, R. J., Frontier, T., & Livingston, D. (2011). *Effective supervision: Supporting the art and science of teaching.* Alexandria, VA: Association for Supervision and Curriculum Development.

Marzano, R. J., Pickering, D. J., & Pollock, J. E. (2001). *Classroom instruction that works: Research-based strategies for increasing student achievement.* Alexandria, VA: Association for Supervision and Curriculum Development.

McGinnis, J. C., Frederick, B. P., & Edwards, R. (1995). Enhancing classroom management through proactive rules and procedures. *Psychology in the Schools, 32*(3), 220–224.

Mendez, L. M. R. (2003). Predictors of suspension and negative school outcomes: A longitudinal investigation. In J. Wald & D. J. Losen (Eds.), *Deconstructing the school-to-prison pipeline* (pp. 17–33). San Francisco: Jossey-Bass.

Mendez, L. M. R., & Knoff, H. M. (2003). Who gets suspended from school and why: A demographic analysis of schools and disciplinary infractions in a large school district. *Education and Treatment of Children, 26*(1), 30–51.

Miltenberger, R. G. (2005). Strategies for measuring behavior change. In L. Bambara & L. Kern (Eds.), *Individualized supports for students with problem behaviors: Designing positive behavior plans* (pp. 107–128.) New York: Guilford.

Musser, E. H., Bray, M. A., Kehle, T. J., Jenson, W. R. (2001). Reducing disruptive behaviors in students with serious emotional disturbance. *School Psychology Review, 30*(2), 294–305.

Musti-Rao, S., & Haydon, T. (2011). Strategies to increase behavior-specific teacher praise in an inclusive environment. *Intervention in School and Clinic, 47*(2), 91–97.

Nansel, T. R., Overpeck, M., Pilla, R. S., Ruan, W. J., Simons-Morton, B., & Scheidt, P. (2001). Bullying behaviors among US youth: Prevalence and association with psychosocial adjustment. *Journal of the American Medication Association, 285*(16), 2094–2100.

Netzel, D. M., & Eber, L. (2003). Shifting from reactive discipline in an urban school district: A change in focus through PBIS implementation. *Journal of Positive Behavior Interventions, 5*(2), 71–79.

Newton, J. S., Horner, R. H., Todd, A. T., Algozzine, R. F., & Algozzine, K. M. (2012). A pilot study of a problem-solving model for team decision making. *Education and Treatment of Children, 35*(1), 25–49.

Noell, G. H., Duhon, G. J., Gatti, S. L., & Connell, J. E. (2002). Consultation, follow-up, and implementation of behavior management interventions in general education. *School Psychology Review, 31*(2), 217–234.

Oliver, R., Wehby, J., & Reschly, D. J. (2011). Teacher classroom management practices: Effects on disruptive or aggressive student behavior. *Campbell Systematic Reviews, 2011*(4).

O'Neill, R. E., Horner, R. H., Albin, R. W., Sprague, J. R., Storey, K., & Newton, J. S. (1997). *Functional assessment and program development for problem behavior: A practical handbook* (2nd ed.). Pacific Grove, CA: Brooks/Cole.

Oregon RTI. (2013). *Oregon RTI handbook: A model and documentation of RTI practices.* Tigard, OR: Author. Accessed at www.oregonrti.org/wp-content/uploads/2013/07/OrRTI_Handbook_2013_draft.docx on December 18, 2014.

Ostrosky, M. M., Jung, E. Y., Hemmeter, M. L., & Thomas, D. (2008). *Helping children understand routines and classroom schedules* (What Works Brief Series, No. 3). Nashville, TN: Center on the Social and Emotional Foundations for Early Learning, Vanderbilt University.

Otieno, T. N., & Choongo, H. (2008). Disruptive behavior: Prevalence, gender, and impact of bullying in schools. *Journal of Intercultural Discipline, 8*, 98–106.

Partin, T. C., Robertson, R. E., Maggin, D. M., Oliver, R. M., & Wehby, J. H. (2010). Using teacher praise and opportunities to respond to promote appropriate student behavior. *Preventing School Failure, 54*(3), 172–178.

Pierce, W. D., & Cameron, J. (2006). *Rewards and intrinsic motivation: Resolving the controversy* (Paperback ed.). Scottsdale, AZ: Information Age.

Raphael, T. E., & Au, K. H. (2005). QAR: Enhancing comprehension and test taking across grades and content areas. *The Reading Teacher, 59*(3), 206–221.

Rathvon, N. (1999). *Effective school interventions: Strategies for enhancing academic achievement and social competence.* New York: Guilford Press.

Reading Rockets. (n.d.). *Exit slips.* Accessed at www.readingrockets.org/strategies/exit_slips on December 2, 2014.

Reinke, W. M., Herman, K. C., & Stormont, M. (2013). Classroom-level positive behavior supports in schools implementing SW-PBIS: Identifying areas for enhancement. *Journal of Positive Behavior Interventions, 15*(1), 39–50.

Reinke, W. M., Lewis-Palmer, T., & Martin, E. (2007). The use of visual performance feedback on teacher use of behavior-specific praise. *Behavior Modification, 31*(3), 247–263.

Reinke, W. M., Lewis-Palmer, T., & Merrell, K. (2008). The classroom check-up: A classwide teacher consultation model for increasing praise and decreasing disruptive behavior. *School Psychology Review, 37*(3), 315–332.

Robers, S., Kemp, J., Truman, J., & Snyder, T. D. (2013). *Indicators of school crime and safety: 2012* (NCES 2013-036/NCJ 241446). Washington, DC: National Center for Education Statistics. Accessed at http://nces.ed.gov/pubs2013/2013036.pdf on December 2, 2014.

Rohrbeck, C. A., Ginsberg-Block, M. D., Fantuzzo, J. W., & Miller, T. R. (2003). Peer-assisted learning interventions with elementary school students: A meta-analytic review. *Journal of Educational Psychology, 95*(2), 240–257.

Ryan, R. M., & Deci, E. L. (2000). Self-determination theory and the facilitation of intrinsic motivation, social development, and well-being. *American Psychologist, 55*(1), 68–78.

Ryan, J. B., Sanders, S., Katsiyannis, A., & Yell, M. L. (2007). Using time-out effectively in the classroom. *Teaching Exceptional Children, 39*(4), 60–67.

Sailor, W., Dunlap, G., Sugai, G., & Horner, R. (Eds.). (2009). *Handbook of positive behavior support.* New York: Springer.

Sheinhorn, A. (2009). *North County High School PBIS presentation.* Presented at PBIS in High Schools: What Works!, Maryland. Accessed at www.pbismaryland.org/Presentations/HSForumNovember2008 /NCHS_PBIS_presentation_11–12.ppt on September 26, 2014.

Simonsen, B., Fairbanks, S., Briesch, A., Myers, D., & Sugai, G. (2008). Evidence-based practices in classroom management: Considerations for research to practice. *Education and Treatment of Children, 31*(3), 351–380.

Simonsen, B., & Freeman, J. (n.d.). *Helping teachers help themselves: Self-management strategies to support teachers' classroom management.* Accessed at www.mayinstitute.org/pdfs/PBIS%20-%20Simonsen -Supporting%20Teachers%20Classroom%20Mgmt%202013%20Handout.pdf on December 2, 2014.

Simonsen, B., Myers, D., & DeLuca, C. (2010). Teaching teachers to use prompts, opportunities to respond, and specific praise. *Teacher Education and Special Education, 33*(4), 300–318.

Simonsen, B., Sugai, G., & Negron, M. (2008). Schoolwide positive behavior supports: Primary systems and practices. *Teaching Exceptional Children, 40*(6), 32–40.

Skiba, R. (2010). Zero tolerance and alternative discipline strategies. *NASP Communique, 39*(1), 28.

Skiba, R., Michael, R. S., Nardo, A. C., & Peterson, R. L. (2002). The color of discipline: Sources of racial and gender disproportionality in school punishment. *The Urban Review, 34*(4), 317–342.

Skiba, R., & Peterson, R. (2000). School discipline at a crossroads: From zero tolerance to early response. *Exceptional Children, 66*(3), 335–346.

Skinner, B. F. (1953). *Science and human behavior.* New York: The Free Press.

Skinner, B. F. (1976). *About behaviorism.* New York: Random House.

Slonski-Fowler, K. E., & Truscott, S. D. (2004). General education teachers' perceptions of the pre-referral intervention team process. *Journal of Education and Psychological Consultation, 15*(1), 1–39.

Stage, S. A., & Quiroz, D. R. (1997). A meta-analysis of interventions to decrease disruptive classroom behavior in public education. *School Psychology Review, 26*(3), 333–368.

Steege, M. W., & Watson, T. S. (2009). *Conducting school-based functional behavioral assessments: A practitioner's guide* (2nd ed.). New York: Guilford Press.

Stormont, M., Smith, S. C., & Lewis, T. J. (2007). Teacher implementation of precorrection and praise statements in Head Start classrooms and as a component of program-wide positive behavioral support. *Journal of Behavioral Education, 16*(3), 280–290.

Stronge, J. H., Ward, T. J., & Grant, L. W. (2011). What makes good teachers good? A cross-case analysis of the connection between teacher effectiveness and student achievement. *Journal of Teacher Education, 62*(4), 339–355.

Stronge, J. H., Ward, T. J., Tucker, P. D., & Hindman, J. L. (2008). What is the relationship between teacher quality and student achievement? An exploratory study. *Journal of Personnel Evaluation in Education, 20*(3/4), 165–184.

Sugai, G., & Colvin, G. (1997). Debriefing: A transition step for promoting acceptable behavior. *Education and Treatment of Children, 20*(2), 209–221.

Sutherland, K. S., Alder, N., & Gunter, P. L. (2003). The effect of varying rates of opportunities to respond to academic requests on the classroom behavior of students with EBD. *Journal of Emotional and Behavioral Disorders, 11*(4), 239–248.

Sutherland, K. S., & Wehby, J. H. (2001). Exploring the relationship between increased opportunities to respond to academic requests and the academic and behavioral outcomes of students with EBD: A review. *Remedial and Special Education, 22*(2), 113–121.

Sutherland, K. S., Wehby, J. H., & Copeland, S. R. (2000). Effect of varying rates of behavior-specific praise on the on-task behavior of students with EBD. *Journal of Emotional and Behavioral Disorders, 8*(1), 2–8.

Taylor-Greene, S., Brown, D., Nelson, L., Longton, J., Gassman, T., Cohen, J., et al. (1997). School-wide behavioral support: Starting the year off right. *Journal of Behavior Education, 7*(1), 99–112.

Theodore, L. A., Bray, M. A., Kehle, T. J., & Jenson, W. R. (2001). Randomization of group contingencies and reinforcers to reduce classroom disruptive behavior. *Journal of School Psychology, 39*(3), 267–277.

Tobin, T., Sugai, G., & Colvin, G. (1996). Patterns in middle school discipline records. *Journal of Emotional and Behavioral Disorders, 4*(2), 82–94.

Todd, A. W., Horner, R. H., & Sugai, G. (1999). Self-monitoring and self-recruited praise: Effects on problem behavior, academic engagement, and work completion in a typical classroom. *Journal of Positive Interventions, 1*(2), 66–76.

Todd, A. W., Horner, R. H., & Tobin, T. (2006). Referral form definitions: Version 4.0. *SWIS Documentation Project.* Eugene: University of Oregon. Accessed at www.pbis.org/common/cms/files/NewTeam /Data/ReferralFormDefinitions.pdf on December 2, 2014.

Treptow, M. A., Burns, M. K., & McComas, J. J. (2007). Reading at the frustration, instructional, and independent levels: The effects on student' reading comprehension and time on task. *School Psychology Review, 36*(1), 159–166.

Trussell, R. P. (2008). Classroom universals to prevent problem behaviors. *Behavior Management, 43*(3), 179–185.

U.S. Department of Education Office for Civil Rights. (2014). *Civil Rights data collection: Data snapshot: School discipline.* Accessed at www2.ed.gov/about/offices/list/ocr/docs/crdc-discipline-snap shot.pdf on December 2, 2014.

VanDerHeyden, A. M., & Witt, J. C. (2008). Best practices in can't do/won't do assessment. In A. Thomas & J. Grimes (Eds.), *Best practices in school psychology V* (pp. 131–140). Bethesda, MD: National Association of School Psychologists.

Vavrus, F., & Cole, K. (2002). "I didn't do nothin'": The discursive construction of school suspension. *The Urban Review, 34*(2), 87–111.

Walker, H. M. (1997). *The acting-out child: Coping with classroom disruption.* Boston: Allyn & Bacon.

Walker, H. M., Ramsey, E., & Gresham, F. M. (2003). *Antisocial behavior in school: Evidence-based practices* (2nd ed.). Belmont, CA: Wadsworth/Thomson Learning.

Wallace, J. M., Goodkind, S., Wallace, C. M., & Bachman, J. G. (2008). Racial, ethnic, and gender differences in school discipline among U.S. high school students: 1991–2005. *The Negro Educational Review, 59*(1/2), 47–62.

Watkins, C., & Slocum, T. A. (2004). The components of Direct Instruction. In N. E. Marchand-Martella, T. A. Slocum, & R. C. Martella (Eds.), *Introduction to direct instruction* (pp. 28–65). Boston: Allyn & Bacon.

Watson, J. B. (1913). Psychology as the behaviorist views it. *Psychological Review, 20,* 158–177.

Whitcomb, S. A., & Merrell, K. W. (2012). *Behavioral, social, and emotional assessment of children and adolescents* (4th ed.). New York: Routledge.

White, V., & White, E. (1990). Writing, not fighting: Student letters as problem-solving in the elementary classroom. *Journal of Teaching Writing, 9*(1), 1–10.

Wolery, M. (2011). Intervention research: The importance of fidelity measurement. *Topics in Early Childhood Special Education, 31*(3), 155–157.

Wolery, M., Bailey, D. B., & Sugai, G. M. (1988). *Effective teaching: Principles and procedures of applied behavior analysis with exceptional students.* Boston: Allyn & Bacon.

Wong, H. K., & Wong, R. T. (2009). *The first days of school: How to be an effective teacher* (4th ed.). Mountain View, CA: Wong Publications.

Yarbrough, J. L., Skinner, C. H., Lee, Y. J., & Lemmons, C. (2004). Decreasing transition times in a second grade classroom: Scientific support for the Timely Transitions Game. In C. H. Skinner (Ed.), *Single subject designs for school psychologists* (pp. 85–107). New York: Hawthorne Press.

INDEX

A

academic performance, impact of class management on, 3–4

acceleration phase, 107, 109–110

action responses, 79–80

active student engagement
See also opportunities to respond
defined, 71

active supervision, 89

Adler, N., 73

agitation phase, 107, 108–109

Akin-Little, K. A., 52

Alberto, P., 87

alpha commands, 100, 101

antecedent, 8, 113
strategies, 103, 104

apology letters, 93

applied behavior analysis (ABA), 7, 8, 9

Archer, A., 75–76

Atkins, M., 12

attrition rates for teachers, 4

B

Bachman, J. G., 5–6

behavioral momentum, 101–102

behavioral narration, 51

behaviorism, 7–9

behaviors, direct instruction of desired, 9–11

behavior sequence, 7–8

behavior-specific praise, 49–52

behavior strategies, 103

beta commands, 100, 101

Bevans, K. B., 4

booster session, 29

Bradshaw, C. P., 4

Bray, M., 60

Briere, D., 72

Briesch, A., 11

Brown, M. S., 4

bullying, statistics on, 3

bump factor, 37–38

C

calm phase, 107, 108

Cameron, J., 52

Campbell, S., 11

Canter, L., 44, 51

chance jar, 60–61

choral responses, 74–75

classroom layouts, 37–40, 46

classroom management, effective
components of, 11–14
importance of, 3–4
proactive approach to, 7–11

cold call, 74

Cole, K. M., 6

Colvin, G., 92, 107

Connell, J. E., 6

consequences, 8
positive and negative use of, 86
strategies, 103, 104

Optimize student achievement
with effective classroom management

 Signature PD Service

Designing Effective Classroom Management PD Workshop

Create a classroom environment that supports student achievement and fosters positive behaviors. This workshop provides teachers and school leaders with an overview of the keys to positive and proactive classroom management, using real-life examples and practical steps for implementation.

You'll learn five research-based principles for effective classroom management, including identifying and teaching classroom expectations and rules, reinforcing expectations, and developing ways to decrease unwanted student behavior.

Learning Outcomes

- Understand five principles of effective classroom management.
- Define and teach classroom expectations and rules.
- Create classroom structure and procedures.
- Learn effective methods for increasing student engagement.
- Reinforce classroom expectations with a range of strategies.
- Manage unwanted behavior using a hierarchy of appropriate responses.

Learn more!
marzanoresearch.com/OnsitePD
888.849.0851